Up With Profits

Up With Profits

Edited by

Robert W. McIntosh, Ph.D.

Pan American World Airways, Inc.
New York 1971

Through the publication of this compendium of educational advice and materials, Pan American World Airways, Inc. wishes to acknowledge the continuing value of the programs of the Institute of Certified Travel Agents, and conjoins with ICTA to mutually promote and advance professionalism in the travel industry.

First Edition: 1971
First Printing

Library of Congress Catalog Card Number: 79-152-840

Standard Book Number: 87582-027-1

MANUFACTURED IN USA

CONTENTS

Chapter 1

The Travel Agency Business

by

James A. Miller, CTC

Robert W. McIntosh, Ph.D.

There are but two ways to up profits for any business: increase profitable sales or reduce operating costs. Simpler said than done, increased profits in the travel business only come to those who desire profit improvement and are willing to work at the achievement of this success measure.

Whether it be increased profitable sales or reduced operating expenses or both, it takes planning and thoughtful analysis. Then it takes concerted, controlled effort to unwaveringly carry out the plans and resolutions decided upon. Profitability planning for travel cannot be done in a vacuum, but wearing blinders to keep aiming at the priorities, once the plans have been established, can be helpful.

This book illuminates key aspects in travel agency operations; it should aid in planning and help in selecting the right "blinders" for the priority operating issues. The starting point is understanding the

1

fundamentals of the industry and putting the service provided by the travel agent, and putting the travel agent himself, into the right perspective, *as the customer sees the travel agent and his services.*

Man-Traveler

Even as *Homo Erectus*, the first true man of 1.2 million years ago traveled from place to place in order to forage for food and for safety and comfort, so modern man travels for necessity as well as in response to urges of pleasure and other motivations. With the increasing ease and relatively low cost of travel, the public's aspiration to travel has steadily grown and the market multiplied over the past several decades.

Man by nature is curious and therefore an explorer. Man is also fun loving and a pleasure seeker. Travel as no other business can, provides both the means and end for these two basic human aspirations.

Demand Growth-Supply Growth

As a growing population becomes more educated and affluent, demand for travel service also grows. Economic theory and application of today's business principles are as obvious and appropriate in travel as they are in any industry of the free world.

Beginning in England more than a hundred years ago, the travel agency business has developed and expanded because customers were willing to pay an appropriate price to those creative and enterprising travel service pioneers who were filling their travel needs and desires.

Since Mr. Thomas Cook's first excursion train (July, 1841) the number of travel agencies and types of services performed have grown remarkably. Travel agents are, of course, now found in all modern countries of the world and also in some that are not so modern. As an indication of the growth of this business in the United States and Canada, there were only about 2,000 travel agency locations in 1955 employing an estimated 10,000 persons. With agency locations in operations now exceeding 8,000 it is estimated that over 35,000 travel agents now augment the specific product sales forces of travel-con-nected companies and organizations.

The public's recognition of the travel agent and his functions has also grown remarkably in the past decade. Whereas the public was

2

vaguely aware of the names of a few well known tour operators and only sometimes was aware of the availability of local travel agency services, the words "travel agent" are now found in virtually all advertisements of public carriers as well as in television and radio commercials, newspaper advertisements, mentioned in magazine articles, newspaper columns and television plays, and are generally recognized and accepted as part of every community complex. Hollywood's production of the movie "If it's Tuesday, this must be Belgium," though in part controversial, contributed to the public identification of travel agents and tour operators. The agency is now recognized as a provider of services as are other important professional and service organizations. We anticipate that this growth and identity trend will continue. The improved recognition of travel agents as key marketing outlets for carriers and other principals is evidence that the functions and services of the travel agent are a requisite to marketing success of these carriers and principals.

Growth and prestige would not have resulted had the public not felt the need for travel agency service *and* had travel agents not been able to turn an adequate profit in providing their service. Future growth will continue to depend on the same factors, but the complexity of the business is perhaps now hundreds of times what it was when Mr. Cook began. Now agents are faced with credit problems, competitive pressures from the very transportation and accommodation suppliers they represent, imposed regulation requirements, and inflationary increases in operating costs. Time will tell what "shake out" results may occur should competition or regulation choke off profit opportunity. As in the days of old, however, the creative and enterprising, with perhaps the help of this book and other training, will emerge as the most handsomely rewarded and satisfied in our industry.

Focusing on the United States and Canada, travel has grown because of a beneficial set of circumstances involving increased population, a general improvement in prosperity and living standards, an increase of individual leisure time, more effective marketing programs, and a vast improvement in the convenience, speed, and cost of transportation to and from most of our communities throughout the world. The resulting sheer volume of travel agency-initiated business has created a proportionate increase in the responsibilities of the individual travel agent.

3

Responsibilities of the Travel Agent

In total a multi-billion dollar industry, within each market area, a travel agency can be responsible for millions of dollars in travel sales annually for thousands of individual clients. Incidental to generating profits, here is a summary of fundamental travel agency responsibilities:

The primary responsibility exists in the *safeguarding and proper application of clients' monies*, coupled with a trust responsibility to properly guard, capably report, and transmit the monies to the travel service companies whose products have been sold. *Sound ethics and financial stability* are a must. Public confidence is absolutely essential and so must there be sound intra-industry responsibility among retailers, wholesalers and carriers.

The whole process involves a need for *proper business organization* by the agent of banking, legal, insurance, and general clerical procedures to safely fulfill both the receiving and disbursement functions.

In simplest form, a travel agency may be primarily an arranger of point-to-point transportation for his clients. Within this area, a travel agency will have a responsibility for *maintaining complete and accurate information* of the services he represents, together with *cost and reservation service facilities* to fulfill his client's wishes.

Additionally, agencies must *budget their sales requirements for ticket stocks, and other travel paper requirements* such as hotel and rent-a-car vouchering materials, travelers checks, tour orders, miscellaneous charges orders, credit card sales and transmittal forms. The responsibility for maintaining such sales supplies is joined by the need to *protect, properly use, and properly report the use of such negotiable papers and the monies such sales represent*. Governmental requirements on *reporting of sales, taxes, payrolls, commissions,* added to the agent's own internal requirements — *making sales projections, evaluating cost of doing business, determining departmental budgets* — are time consuming and costly in themselves, but must be fulfilled in order to see where the business is going as well as to comply with the law.

Obviously, even in simplest form, a travel agent will have a responsibility to himself, his clients, his business associates, the companies he represents, and government units for *an accounting*

4

system which satisfies the various normal and special requirements he will encounter in the operation of a travel agency business.

In assuming a full travel agency service posture, the travel agent becomes *responsible for a vast complex of world travel arrangements*

for his clients. The skill and knowledge he must acquire, maintain, and apply in the sales and arrangement of such travel details become a true measure of the agent's competence. As services expand, improvement, upgrading and usually enlargement become necessary, and in so doing the value to oneself, community, and the overall travel industry becomes proportionately greater in importance and scope.

Successful travel agency management today must be alert, well informed, knowledgeable, and *willing to change and improve* in order to do the job better. Successful travel agents sense their responsibility to continually seek to improve their abilities through study, seminars, meetings, discussions with colleagues, familiarization trips, and not infrequently from client opinions and reports on their experiences. A considerable amount of reading becomes a normal agent habit.

Relating to his staff, the travel agency owner or manager is *responsible for employee motivation and development* so that the clients will receive best possible satisfaction. An example of this is the need to provide educational growth opportunity for each office employee — a *planned* experience in training and in familiarization trips which will create the enthusiastic, intelligent counselor who is genuinely motivated to render superior service, and will thereby inevitably increase sales.

The travel agency business often seems to rotate on an alphabetical axis: ASTA, ARTA, ABTB, AAA, IATA, ICTA, CTOA, UFTAA, ACT, CAB. Even hotel plans are AP, MAP or EP, and cities are known by their coded names. Pity the poor typist! One slip and the agent has enrolled in another association, or the passenger goes to another city. The various conferences/congresses/regulatory agencies define travel operations to a great degree, however, and they not only dictate scheduling, fares, ticketing and charters, but even the amounts of office space to be used for stated purposes. *Adherence to rules of membership* and equally to local, state and federal regulations provides a built-in ethic for the industry.

Not a Simple or an Easy Life

Travel is glamourous, exciting, romantic, adventuresome and refreshing: to the would-be traveler. Outside of the industry travel has great appeal and marvelous connotations. But on the operating side of the desk, the travel agency business is in reality a frequently grueling, thankless job, filled with "busy" work. Counselors spend endless hours on paper work which seemingly could be drastically reduced. Agents continually must explain illogical air fares and accommodation prices. Too frequently customers are difficult, shop without earnest intent, and are unbelievably fickle, demonstrated by the number of changes they request and the reasons for such changes.

Customer demands on the retailer's time are not infrequently compounded by harassment in the form of client-initiated law suits or threats of law suits. There are airlines slow to make refunds, tour operators canceling out at the last minute or not delivering what was promised, and credit card companies, whose computers don't respond to inquiries about credit for unused portions of tickets charged on their cards. Then there are the rate, tax and commission calculations invariably requested by some boss or regulatory authority.

The travel agency business requires a lot of office housekeeping on the part of all employees, plus endless reading and filing to "stay current" on information perhaps never to be used.

Agencies going bankrupt are not uncommon, students become stranded in Europe, and even the enormous air carriers and steamship lines seem to suffer acute economic pains through much of their existence.

And the pressures grow from new competitors as well. By their communications facilities, number of well located, high traffic offices and personnel availability, firms far removed from travel or transportation are increasingly disposed to market travel products and services in their quest for growth and operating efficiencies. Banks, insurance companies, stock brokerages and chain department stores offer some of this new competition. Competition is good, or is never all bad; but the race for the necessary sales dollars is distressingly tighter. Agents must not merely keep up, but must stay ahead by using all the creativity and business tools at their disposal.

Anyone who thinks travel is a Garden of Eden industry should reconsider. The trick is to understand the realities of the industry and know what you're doing. A good place to begin understanding this business is to know where sales and profits come from. Your own market area analysis, and your own internal operations cost analysis are essential here, but as a broad gauge starting point, the Department of Commerce report on travel agency receipts is very helpful.

Agencies which supplied information to the Bureau of the Census on the source of their receipts in the 1967 study indicated that air travel accounted for more than 64 per cent of gross sales, with domestic travel almost 2/3 of that total, or more than 40 per cent; international sales accounted for the remaining 24 per cent. The next largest sales came from packaged tours — almost 16 per cent. Steamship travel made up 10 per cent of sales and all other sources, including rail, bus, car rental and lodging accounted for the remaining 10 per cent.

To emphasize the need for further analysis, despite the large portion of sales coming from air transportation arrangements, some agents have ceased handling domestic flight ticketing because it costs them more to provide the service than they can receive in compensation for it. Some service, they argue, can be provided at a loss to obtain other more profitable business. Every business is entitled to just rewards for service rendered. In our free enterprise system, each business is free to determine what products or services it will offer, and what rewards it considers "just" for providing these products or services. By their purchases, the market of customers will determine if the business' selection of product offerings and price is, after all, acceptable.

Characteristics of the Professional Travel Agent

Competent, professional travel counseling demands wide travel experiences, sales and agency experience. An educational academic background pertaining to the disciplines most relating to travel is also helpful. These disciplines include practical knowledge of fine arts, such as painting, sculpture, architecture, and music; and history, archeology and cultural and physical geography.

A knowledge and practice of interpersonal psychology is also extremely useful, especially in sales and conducting efficient conversations with clients to bring out their true or complete interests and needs. With good communications and understanding, a travel agent can best offer suggestions for a trip, complementary to the client, which provide important values that would not have been possible without the assistance of the travel counselor.

The travel agency provides two primary services to the public: 1. *Selling tickets and providing other travel services* to those persons who wish to travel to a pre-determined destination and probably by an already decided mode of transportation; and 2. *Individual personal counseling* to those persons who are considering a more complex travel experience in which many factors are unknown and who are in need of competent counsel. The first requires principally courtesy, efficient and accurate detail work, and then proper reporting, accounting and similar routine functions. The second, however, is much different. This function of the travel agent is the true professional one. Here the competent travel counselor provides advice which is essential to the

8

fulfillment of his client's travel expectations. Such competent advice often provides a new dimension to the trip which immeasurably adds to its value and pleasure.

Sometimes counseling is a matter of comforting jittery first time flyers; sometimes countering a traveler's fear of being hijacked and explaining precautions taken to prevent it. Often this advice takes the form of special knowledge — of language, or a correspondent in another country, even knowledge of information sources: membership lists of associations with chapters abroad, available in most large libraries; consular and foreign trade attache personnel; Department of Commerce field office staff and library facilities. This creative and challenging aspect of the travel agency business attests to its professional status.

The travel agent should expect to be recognized as a respected and valued member of his business and professional communities. Thus, it is important for him to maintain good public relations and to enjoy a reputation of providing valuable services to the community. The travel agent should have as much prestige as any other businessman or professional person in the community. Pictures and stories in local newspapers carry the story of the good works of the travel agent to the public, helping to build his reputation and beneficial influence in the local markets.

The Future Looks Most Promising

The travel industry today abounds in growth potentials. Only slightly over half of all U.S. families take an annual (or more frequent) vacation away from home and only 15 per cent of all travel is by public carrier. The present U.S. travel expenditure is about $36 billion, which constitutes but 5 to 6 per cent of our disposable income. Leading economists seem to agree that powerful economic and social forces now encourage a rapid potential growth of leisure and the desire (and means) to use this leisure for travel. Modern technology will increase worker productivity, for example, and this will increase his leisure time. Exciting potentials exist for the expansion of travel markets in the youth, family, older person and special interest group segments. A $40 billion, or larger market should be attainable by 1980 as the economy gradually expands and the travel industry agressively cultivates and develops its markets. The advent of a more secure world peace may have the result of accelerating the expansion timetable beyond even the current expectations.

The travel agent's share of this expanding market should greatly increase as public carriers move ahead with their mass transport technological problems and solutions. The individual traveler will no doubt gladly accept the new efficiencies of larger and faster transport units, but he will probably still desire the personal attention and competent local counsel available through his travel agent to best satisfy his total travel objectives.

In this era of economic specialization, in many cities, the staffs of the various airline companies have grown but little, or not at all in the past 10 years. But the travel agencies in these cities have expanded their staffs many times and new agencies and branches of agencies have now or will shortly come into being.

Comparative statistics indicate a continually growing share of the travel market by travel agents. In a 9 year period (1960-1969) one major domestic air carrier's passenger sales increased a dramatic 285 percent, but for this same period, sales by this carrier's agents increased 414 per cent! This gain also reflected a 32 per cent increase in the proportion of travel agency sales to total passenger sales. Estimated travel agency manpower increased only 250 per cent in this same period. Growth indication would suggest that by 1980, at least 50 per cent of all passenger sales for this carrier will be processed through travel agents.

If this carrier's growth continues at the same pace, in 1980 the dollar sales through travel agents of this one airline's product will be greater than all travel agency domestic air ticket sales for the year 1967, and will exceed $1,000,000,000.

Population growth alone insures an expanded market, but the expanding market is increasingly segmented. Tour operators, appreciating the value of segmentation, create new packages to appeal to the diverse interests of potential traveling customers. Student travel, explorer travel, high volume-low budget, low volume-high budget, singles only, senior citizens, specific country or area specialities, fly/cruise and open jaw routing appeal to many differing groups.

10

Customers Are Key

As with any business, nothing happens and no revenues are generated until a sales transaction takes place; until a client or customer says "Yes, I will use your product or service," and exchanges cash for receipt of that product or service. And, of course, it takes two parties to make the sales transaction: you, the supplier, and the purchasing party, the customer.

The overall marketing objectives for a travel agency are generally clear enough: attract and repeatedly serve as many customers as possible, consistent with good service. Good service is essential in order for a customer to return and become a loyal repeat purchaser. By clever or expensive promotion, you might attract a customer initially, but if he does not receive good service (satisfactory value) for his purchase, he will not be attracted to buy from you again.

With a limited number of potential customers in each market area and the usually high promotional costs to attract new customers, an agency business inevitably has to be built on repeat customers or financial viability will not exist.

Loyalty on the part of the client toward his travel agent can be built in the same way that loyalty to any other professional person is developed. Success leads to greater success and not only will the satisfied client return to his favorite travel agent again and again, but he will recommend his friends and associates do so as well. People like to "share the good news" and are confident that their friends will receive the same attention and competent service they have themselves enjoyed and appreciated.

Summation

Indeed, travel agents have become a major element in the marketing of transportation for public carriers and all of the attendant facilities and services now commonly recognized and embraced in the word, *travel.* Travel agents now assume prominence in the operations of transportation carriers, the hotel, motel and resort industry, local service transportation companies, railroads, steamship companies and all levels of governments. Tourism development potentials in foreign countries, organizations concerned with travel facilitation and world organizations dealing with international law are now achieving some recognition in the field of formal educational processes because of the massive flow of customers and travel dollars which this burgeoning industry produces. About 1/3 of all domestic air transportation sales are made through travel agents. About 90 per cent of all cruises, and about substantially over half of all international air travel sales are attributable to travel agents. Total agency sales amount to several billion dollars annually and thus, travel agencies are a most vital link in the travel marketing process. Net receipts to travel agents representing commissions and other operating revenues total more than $300 million. With some 8,000 retail travel agency locations in the United States and Canada, a network of sales offices has been created which couldn't possibly be provided by any single principal or group of principals.

Travel agents expect to assume a growing future responsibility for developing new markets, servicing an increasingly larger proportion of the market, and a growing total volume of sales. In turn, the carriers and other travel firms expect their travel agencies to function as prime marketing and sales outlets for the total travel package. These principals are counting on their appointed travel agents to increase their marketing responsibilities and have growing expectations of the agents' performance and constantly improving abilities.

The preparation of this manual is an example of a contribution by a major carrier to the growth of the travel agents' educational resources. It is intended to assist the agent in meeting the goals and aspirations of both the carrier and the travel agent by providing ideas and progressive management principles for their mutual benefit. Hopefully, the end result will prove extremely attractive to the traveling public.

For the travel agency, profit improvement per se will come from thoughtful analyses, accurate planning and diligent follow-through. This book channels constructive thought and offers guidelines for action, specifically pointed toward marketing improvement and more efficient operations. When it is all said and done, profitable sales will have been increased, or operating expenses reduced, or both — or no profit improvement will have been achieved. Application and results are up to you.

Chapter 2

Office Layout and Appearance

by

Carl Massara, A.I.A.

Planning for Your Business

Because there are many different factors involved in shaping the personality of each travel agency organization... business volume, personnel, location and clientele, the office layout and physical needs of each agency will vary considerably. However, there are certain basic characteristics common to all travel agencies which must be considered, such as office location, necessary professional services, and guidelines for function and design. These will be discussed in this chapter. Particular attention will be given to the layout of large and small offices, spatial requirements and the creation of efficient, spacious and attractive work situations. The author's design of the Rosenbluth Travel Agency will be developed at the end of the chapter as a typical example of procedures necessary in the architectural considerations of the travel agency business. Here, space problems were solved both aesthetically and profitably.

13

The location of your agency was primarily determined because that's where your business was, or the cost of operation came within your budget. Given a choice of a new office location, or remodeling the present one, you must, of course, consider the type of travel business in which you are now engaged or which you prefer to handle. If your business is general in nature, the advantages of a location in a central area where potential and actual clients may conveniently stop by during the working day to arrange business and personal travel plans and easily pick up tickets, are obvious.

In choosing a location, you must also remember the complementary services which you should be near, such as consulates, cruise lines and other business or governmental operations, or large industrial or corporate accounts, whose proximity is important to you. Do the advantages of being in a bustling, far-out shopping plaza outweigh the inconveniences of being readily available to and in the midst of your principle market? These and other questions must be answered before you sign a new lease.

Regardless of the type of agency work in which you intend to specialize, you cannot forget the principle that the larger the office, the more diversified the personnel will be and, hence, the more planning needed for layout and appearance.

Role of the Architect

Complete coordination of office space needs and effective interior design are highly specialized fields. The fee for a qualified architect will prove to be an economical investment in the long run. Such services will help you to remodel or select a good location, analyze your space needs, project future space requirements and create an organized total environment, which conveys a unified image for an agency notable as a positive and effective environment.

When selecting an architect, previous experience and reputation for excelling in work dealing with office spaces, particularly work for travel agencies, should be investigated. Have similar jobs been supervised satisfactorily within the budget which was set up? The architect should submit a proposal regarding his methods of designing and executing his layout. He should outline the proposed planning stages and design models with which he plans to demonstrate his design concepts. Does he plan to demonstrate alternate design schemes in model form? The architect should also make clear how he plans to communicate with you through all of the design phases. Will he submit time sheets, progress sheets, projections of man hours used within the budget allowance? Of course, he will also review both the ATC and IATA requirements regarding a travel agency's location, premises, dimensions and appearance.

An experienced, competent architect has many specialists on his staff, or on a consulting basis, whom he can call on, depending upon the complexity of the job. After the architect creates the basic spatial design, he then works closely with his specialists on the particulars of your job. For instance, under the guidance of the architect, the structural engineer suggests additional approaches for the structural design or renovation of the building or office, such as using relatively inexpensive materials which afford many new and exciting design possibilities. The architect's mechanical engineer is able to unobtrusively transform the mechanical equipment of the building (heating, lighting and air conditioning) into the total aesthetic design. The interior design specialist will suggest colors, textures and furnishings from his extensive, current samples of wall and floor coverings, paint samples and furniture. Of course, the designer will be able to supply you with the prices of all of the products you choose and will be on hand at the time of their installation to make sure that they are properly placed and beautifully arranged. Where appropriate, the landscape architect, another specialist, will coordinate the exterior of your building with its interior to carry through the total beautiful impression you are striving for. And, as needed, the graphics specialist develops an overall design and image for the travel agency to present its name to the public, such as symbols used throughout the agency office, a distinctive sculpture, an impressive entrance door, and right on through to a memorable logo and letterheads. Lighting and acoustical engineers articulate spaces through the dramatic use of lights and can effectively cut off noise from the outside and suggest ways in which light and sound can make it easier to effectively conduct business within the office. All of these various consultants will work under the guidance and supervision of the architect and may be included in his fee.

Your Agency and Regulations

Before you can open a branch or an agency in a new location, you must make sure that the proposed location is zoned commercially. If any renovations or alterations are contemplated, then usually one must consult the local building codes. These codes generally require that a building permit be obtained from the county or city building, planning or standards inspection department before any work commences. Building codes normally deal with the safety and welfare of the public.

Travel agencies must also comply with the rules set up for the members of IATA and ATC. Briefly, IATA regulations require that the premises be:

a) a place of business exclusively devoted to the promotion and sale of passenger transportation and related services,

b) the agency must have its own entrance separated from other offices by the use of permanent partitions that are high enough to clearly delineate the area,

c) partitions are to be in keeping with the surrounding décor,

d) area must be clearly identifiable as a travel agency.

   ATC regulations are very similar to IATA's, including:

a) that agencies meet reasonable standards for agencies as to dimensions and appearance,

b) agency to be identified by permanent signs both inside and outside. If within an office building, they should be listed on the building's directory,

c) display racks should display promotional material and tour folders,

d) it is desirable to have a display window.

Although IATA and ATC rule requirements are very general, they do establish some minimum standards in terms of guidelines for the travel agent.

Location in City

Proper location of a travel agency is of vital importance for its effective work. First of all, an effective position is a central one where there would be heavy traffic and a gathering point of different human interests. However, being in the center of the city is not the only condition for the success of a travel agency. The atmosphere and character of some part of the city or of a street is of equal importance. Nowadays, we can follow a trend dictating that travel agencies, as well as airline or other agencies, are located in the same area or on the same street, thus forming a specialized market of travel or holiday possibilities. In this way people interested could choose between different offerings, compare prices, suitability of arrangements, etc. An agency located out of such a "travel market" may experience less business.

The overall characteristic of the part of the city where the travel agencies tend to locate should have more shopping than business characteristics — a fun and entertainment atmosphere. Yet, it should not be in a noisy or bad area in terms of the local social profile. A travel agency belongs in a sophisticated section of activities. A typical suitable position is near hotels, clubs, restaurants, smart shops, and so on. We can see now or ahead in the near future that a good location of a travel agency would be in the shopping center of a neighborhood, serving the travel needs of the people living nearby.

Traffic Situation

If we consider the suitability of the location of an agency in terms of the urban form, then the fluidity of the traffic situation is important. Adequate parking facilities, as well as interesting walkways with parks, plazas, etc. are necessary. A leisurely area tends to make people think about travel possibilities. Pleasant and pedestrian traffic helps to create this mood.

Location and Urban Form

The normal places and ambients where people gather, as well as main points of interest that attract tourists, will attract a flow of people to the travel agency. In these terms travel agencies could be located at popular tourist points within or outside the city. The travel agent should do everything to help improve the urban surroundings or landscape around the agency. Interesting materials for walkways, seating facilities, aesthetic design of signs, choice of colors, are all important in creating the proper urban form for an agency.

As far as the location of a travel agency in the building is concerned, the first or ground floor offers much more advantages than would any other floor. Should the agency expand to more floors, the main entrance, waiting area and general sales should remain on the first floor, while secondary functions and supporting facilities could be located on upper or lower floors.

Space and Function

Concerning the space and form, we must ask ourselves what do people expect from a travel agency. These days, image is often an overworked word, but a lot of value remains in its meaning and application to the travel agency business. Take a survey of your friends and ask them what thoughts the words "travel agency" conjure up in their minds. More than likely their replies will include the phrases: exciting place, exotic lands, unique qualities, contemporary facilities. But most important, you'll find that a travel agency should impart confidence, capability and professionalism. It and its staff should convey the impression of successful trips, smoothly arranged.

Can an image convey excitement, spontanaiety and fun while at the same time seem highly expeditious and businesslike? It can be done. A good approach is to use a progressive series of moods as one passes through the office portal into the business area.

1. Entrance, Browsing and Reception Areas

The entrance is a psychological conditioner regardless of the type of building or facility. It can create a mood of excitement. It can break the ice, making one feel free to request information and communicate

18

travel desires. It's important to create an intermediate space, no matter how limited your means, between the exterior, the busy street, and the interior of the agency. Here in such a shelter, people can stop and look at the displays without being distracted by passersby, and can receive some travel information. This intermediate space, as well as the entrance itself, should to the largest extent express the excitement of travel.

The reception-browsing area is the next physical encounter and psychological space. Now the impact upon the client is much more exact and direct. This area should impart the atmosphere of the agency. Here the prospective client has his first contact with agency personnel. Any hesitancy about seeking information must be overcome to prevent him from leaving the area before asking some questions or for some information. The browsing area should contain brochures which are neatly arranged and easily accessible so that the prospective client does not feel obligated or self-conscious. In a larger agency, there could be periodic exhibits of interest, creating an added interest or attraction to the atmosphere of travel.

Depending upon the size of your agencies, you may want to encourage or discourage browsers from talking to your sales people. If you are a small agency, more than likely you will want to be on a friendly basis with anyone who comes through the door. However, experience has taught owners of large agencies that often browsers are killing time at the expense of their salespeople. Therefore, a definite shield can be developed to forestall people with such motives.

2. Sales Area

The way to successfully "screen" people is not to locate your work force within immediate range. The sales people should be separated from the reception area either physically – by putting them on a slightly different level – or through the use of furnishings or plant arrangement.

Once in the actual area devoted to salespeople in the travel department, the client should be impressed with a friendly, yet organized arrangement where business transactions are made. At this point a feeling that this is a serious and reliable operation must be immediately conveyed.

Desks and personnel should be arranged according to profit possibilities. High volume, low cost trips should be sold at the front of this section. This way the agency will look busy and clients will be able to get in and out quickly. Cruises and more expensive vacations should be handled in the back sections of the office where the hustle and bustle is kept to a minimum and expensive arrangements can be planned. At least a 4' space between desks is recommended.

Supervisory persons should be located so that they have an overall view of both the people entering the agency and of the personnel who work with clients. Clients and personnel should be aware of the presence of the boss at all times.

3. Support Functions

What we have discussed so far are the areas generally seen by the public. However, there are other necessary working areas, such as the mail section, conference room, accounting section, ticketing department and other "non-sales" sections.

The mail section can be a small space centrally located so that incoming mail can be readily distributed to the various departments. It should be located near the central brochure filing system to enable the speedy handling of requests for brochures and the filing of incoming brochures. The mail section should also be physically near the accounting department because so much mail is generated between these two points.

The accounting department should also be centrally located so as to handle the financial transactions quickly. Besides the standard adding machines and typewriters included in this area, a safe should be installed to hold all valuable unissued travel tickets and cash, plus any valuable documents the organization might have. If your airline ticket volume is high, you should elect to have a separate and secure place for storing unissued tickets.

A conference room or area is useful for special meetings with clients or staff. It need not be a definite and separate space, but it could be a subdivision of the browsing-reception area. The room or area should be so arranged as to accommodate itself to slide shows and special promotions or projects, as may be required.

If your agency is large enough to also have an airline department, it

20

should be located in a less public area, because many people merely obtaining airline tickets will probably call for reservations on the phone. If the client is booking a tour, the salesperson will order the airline tickets from the airline department directly and will receive the tickets himself. In a small travel agency, ticketing functions will probably be handled by one person working in a small space.

4. Office Security

Principals of the agency should exercise reasonable care in maintaining agency security. There are many types of security systems — some work on a basis of light rays, others work when a metallic wire is broken, others by pressure such as walking, and still others by noise. These systems can be connected to a local police station or a burglar alarm agency. A monthly fee is charged. Whether or not you are contemplating the installation of a burglar alarm system, it is suggested that you contact a reliable agency to check your premises. This consultation service is generally free of charge and will at least point out the weak points of penetration. Sometimes, merely an additional lock at that point will solve your problem.

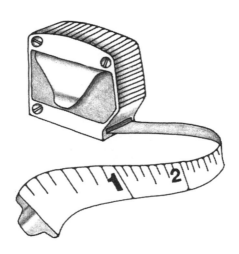

A fire alarm system should also be investigated. Fire detectors can be located in the ceiling. These are triggered when a particular intensity of heat is reached.

Organization of Space, Flexibility and Growth

Growth, the key to business success, should be taken into account. Therefore, many changes will probably be occurring within your organization. A major consideration in planning office space today is flexibility. This goes doubly for the travel agency business. Not only are economics involved in flexible planning, but there is a tendency for an agency to expand over a period of time without having additional available space. Just as important, the travel market is constantly changing, causing priorities in business directions to change.

Spatial Requirements

The first step in creating flexible spaces is to determine what the spatial requirements are.

Following is a list of recommended items and sizes related to travel agency design:

1. The minimum size of a private office should be no less than 6'6"x 8' and if it is this small, its partitions should be made of glass to create a feeling of spaciousness.

2. The mail section should have a 2' x 6' to 8' long working surface with drawers for storing various mailroom paraphernalia. One drawer should be equipped with a lock. This drawer will hold the postage meter and other valuable items when not in use. A tack board should be included in this area for posting information; also, a few shelves should be provided for the storage of brochures until they are filed.

3. Depending upon the size of the office, two typing desks should be included. In a very small office, the typing might be done by the person who sells. However, it is best to centrally locate a typing area with a secretary who does all of the general typing for all of the sales

people. At this point analyze the proposed storage system in general. Is it a system that makes everything easy to find? Is it easy for all to comprehend? If not, revise it before building a design around it! (Remember, coat racks and storage units are important in both warm and cold climates.)

4. The number of central filing cabinets needed in an office is generally determined by the number of people. For the general files used by the sales staff at large, allow 4 file drawers per person, i.e. 7 sales people — 28 file drawers. Each sales person should also have 2 file drawers for his own personal files, regarding office business that accumulates over a period of time.

   There are many different types of filing cabinets. Lateral files are 36" and 42" wide and are 18" deep. They can be desk height to 65" high. Lateral files have been known to be highly workable in many offices, because they look like furniture and work nicely in narrow office space.

5. Your layout should also include separate toilet rooms for men and women wherever possible. The number of fixtures in each bathroom is determined by law and should be investigated by you or your architect. Generally, you provide one water closet for every 15 employees of each sex.

Subdivisions of Space

Organize your space in terms of current functions and activities. Spatial enclosure for various functions is necessary, but it need not be of the solid-walled variety. Psychological tests have proved that such enclosed spaces are not conducive to activity nor productivity. Spatial enclosure should allow for concentration, yet permit communication, mobility and stimulating interaction.

Dividers can serve many functions. For example, systems are available whereby storage and files for working material can be hung on movable wall panels. A variety of shelves, work surfaces, display panels, communication carrels can be integrated into an aesthetic, pragmatic system which articulates the working areas as well. Thus, partitions support working equipment and furnishings while providing a sense of private working territory for each employee, and enabling a great amount of floor space to be reclaimed. The environment of each employee becomes a base indicating who he is and what type of work he specializes in. Work-in-progress becomes a form of display.

Cramped spatial needs can also be alleviated by multi-function areas. A likely candidate for such a multi-use area is the conference area. For example, a reception area can be converted when necessary into a conference area by a folding partition which would separate it from other areas while a conference is in progress. Also, a lounge area (to encourage workers to eat in and perhaps take shorter luncheon breaks) could also double for a conference area.

Supervision

Efficiency is also a major consideration when one is laying out an office. A good control system must be devised, one which will structure work expectations. Visible supervision should be physically apparent to every employee. Such supervision is also important for office training. Working spaces should allow for interaction and training without excessive movement between uninvolved working spaces. Such commotion wastes time and disturbs others.

Coffee Break

Another problem in efficiency planning is the much-heralded coffee break. Long coffee breaks are facilitated by the waiting period before the coffee arrives. An area which provides a small, low maintenance, self-service kitchen where people can prepare their own coffee as they want it cuts out the waiting period and also serves to stagger the breaks.

Inner Circulation

Another critical consideration in office layout is circulation. While a sense of engrossing productivity is stimulating, improperly routed traffic between various functions is confusing. When production is interrupted by cross-cutting and unrelated traffic, activity will soon break down into utter chaos. Anticipated routes of employees as well as customers should be projected so that the final executed layout will offer no surprises in the area of circulation.

Construction and Remodeling

New Construction

When choosing the type of construction for a new building, we must consider the ability to accommodate later changes. In this respect, a skeleton structure — either of concrete or steel — is far more desirable than the bearing wall type. Large, uninterrupted space is more adaptable to change than a narrow one. The space of an agency should be considered as a container within which any changes of spatial subdivisions can be later realized. Floor and ceiling construction should enable the installation of partitions to occur readily. If possible, the height of the ceiling should be such as to allow the user to install a mezzanine if the need for additional space arises. The ceiling should be designed so that the light fixtures can be easily relocated. Also, in the event that any of the equipment such as plumbing, heating, ventilation, electrical wires, or telephone, needs repairing, this can be easily accomplished. Plumbing lines should be so located as to easily enable future additions of toilets, service sinks, and other facilities.

Remodeling

Often office spaces require substantial remodeling. This is more often the case if one selects a central city location. Such a space presents special design problems. For instance, modern mechanical equipment must be unobtrusively and inexpensively fit into the older facility. One solution is to lower the ceiling to accommodate the new lighting and other mechanical necessities, such as air conditioning and heating. The result is that spatial areas can be defined while solving practical needs. A lowered ceiling can create a contrast between receptive and more businesslike spaces.

Another problem with older construction, usually, is that certain awkward, no longer useful features predominate. Unnatural geometric features or proportions are often encountered in older spaces which have in the process of time been chopped down from still larger spaces. One solution is to turn an ungainly feature into an asset. For example, if a ceiling is disproportionately high, this could be emphasized by hanging lights from the vertical space, using tall plants, emphasizing

25

columns, using vertical strips of color or wood panels. The verticality could then be countered by contrasting horizontals for furniture, railings, partitions, etc. Conversely, if horizontals predominate in a monotonous fashion, verticals could be used as a welcome contrast and relief.

When initially inspecting a location, special attention should be paid to the existing wiring, walls, ceilings and floor construction. An old fuse box, old light fixtures and old wires might indicate old wiring which could be a fire hazard. Peeling paint with water spots might mean water is coming through the walls, or a high humidity area. Cracks in the walls often foretell of structural problems. Squeaky and bouncy floors can indicate poor floor construction.

Check the air-conditioning system, if there is one, to see that it is adequate to keep your clients and employees comfortable. Factors that determine the size of the air-conditioning system are as follows: volume of spaces, insulation of floors, walls and roofs, the number of windows and doors, and whether or not they are insulated and weatherproofed, and the anticipated number of people. A rule of thumb is that one ton of air-conditioning is required to cool 325 square feet to 425 square feet of floor space, depending upon the above factors. If heavy traffic is expected in and out of the building — which would mean a constant opening and closing of doors — a vestibule is recommended with its own separate air current.

Interior Design

The personality of your travel agency should express itself especially in the outside of the building, the entranceway, and in the arrangement of the window displays. The browsing area should feature vivid colors and exotic displays. Yet, the total atmosphere should be calm, conveying a mood of reliability and friendliness.

Materials

Attention should be paid to the materials used in the creation of the office design. Materials should be used which form lively spaces and reflect the spirit of 20th century technology.

26

The nature and the expression of the material should always be felt. For example, plastic is a highly sculptural material. Its transparency and lightness make it highly conducive to producing a sense of airiness and spaciousness.

Lacquered wood and chrome also reflect light and give a sense of spaciousness. Glass is another effective material. For example, glass partitions provide for both acoustical privacy and visual continuity. With a glass partition, light from the window in a separate working area can be borrowed for a working space. Mirrors which reflect light and give great senses of space can be used in many ingenious ways.

Another factor which can be considered in giving a sense of spaciousness is the floor treatment. Shiny surface materials, such as tile or wood, will reflect light although they do not absorb noise. Carpeting can be used to improve acoustical privacy in the business area.

Floors

Concerning the materials used for floor areas, we know that traffic will be much heavier in the reception-browsing areas than in the more specialized or general office areas. This area will call for the use of a more durable material, such as vinyl, quarry or ceramic tiles. As these materials are more of a cooler nature, we should use colors such as terra cotta, brown, warm gray, etc.

Carpeting should be used in the offices. The best for these purposes is commercial grade with rubber backing. In certain other areas, such as lavatories, lunch or coffee areas, where there is an extensive amount of water being used, we should again use materials which guard against water such as mosaic, quarry tile, ceramic tile, etc.

Windows

As already mentioned, fixed windows are best for air-conditioning as well as being a good precautionary measure in terms of security. For a better and more economic operation of air-conditioning systems, an insulated glass is very useful. We can obtain a more private and intimate atmosphere with a gray or brown tinted glass. Wire glass should be used, where not seen by the public, to discourage people from breaking in.

Lighting

Factors that determine the amount of light fixtures required are:

1) The number and size of outside windows,
2) Interior colors,
3) Orientation,
4) Vicinity of nearby buildings and their shadows,
5) Size and height of space.

The browsing area should be well lit with general fluorescent lighting. Special displays in this area should be accented with some 150-watt spotlights. General fluorescent lighting fixtures come in 2-tube and 4-tube lights. And the same fixtures are designed to fit in a hung ceiling; others can be surface mounted on existing ceilings. The general size of these fixtures is 2' x 4'. Light fixtures should not be spaced more than 8' to 10' on-center; or, the distance between light fixtures should not exceed the distance between floor and ceiling, whichever is smaller.

Let us now consider the design of lighting: Luminescent or light coverings on windows emit light and add to fresh, open atmosphere, if one is lucky enough to have windows with open views. Plant materials, of course, always lend a feeling of light and airiness to a room.

Lighting should be planned with flexibility in mind. For example, general fixtures can be installed so that the ceiling need not be disturbed to accommodate a future plan. Light control can also be installed from key switch points rather than from individual switches for each office area.

Given the fact that one's spatial needs, whether due to economics or expansion, are often cramped, it is important to create a sense of spaciousness and a unified décor within the total office space. As has been pointed out, lighting is a very important feature in the office design. It can create atmosphere as well as give illumination. Spots can be used to wash or highlight given areas. Recessed "down" lights can be used to emphasize an object or a space. Much has been done in recent years with kinetic lighting. Lights changing color patterns and/or flashing on and off can do much to create exciting and interesting effects.

Colors, Partitions, Furniture

Levels can be used to determine spaces, retaining a sense of openness at the same time. A double-height space can convey a sense of welcome while a lowered space can convey a sense of seclusion.

At times, glass partitions which have curtains that can be drawn are necessary. They afford a sense of fluid space while at the same time offering privacy when desired. By this means, office activity becomes part of the general officescape while a partial curtain lends a degree of quiet and privacy.

Partitions of wood and translucent glass, giving psychological and some visual separation, are also good space dividers. Planters too make good psychological space dividers. Free-standing storage can partition corridors.

Color can also be used to define areas or give spatial emphasis. It can also be used to break up long corridors. Splashes of color enliven the dullest spaces. Light colors can be used to create a greater sense of spaciousness. Colors can be used to tie together a design scheme, creating a feeling that the office is a single extended unit, rather than small separated work spaces.

Flexibility can also be promoted in the selection of office furniture. Modular furniture with changeable components is available. Furniture with wheels facilitates flexible spatial arrangements. Also, attractive folding or stacking chairs which can be easily stored have great utility.

Aside from office décor, such as plants, furniture, paintings and the like, a unique and individual opportunity for decoration is offered by using one's own accomplishments, such as framed awards, degrees, pictures of employees in foreign lands, tour groups, and similar personal touches.

Plants

Decorative plants in the office and especially in the browsing area would enhance the vivid and "open to the public" atmosphere of the

29

agency. Exotic, tropical and rare plants will remind clients of the charm
of faraway places.

Displays

Brochure racks should be placed in an interesting and variant style
and at the same time in a visible and easily accessible place in harmony
with the whole interior. The tables or special arrangements of the
seating facilities should also include brochure racks. All displays, such
as inscriptions, titles, graphics, etc., should be harmoniously designed.
Special displays in larger offices can be used in an area where color
slides or movie projections are sometimes used.

A Four-Person Office

A typical layout is shown in Plan I. The functional division of the
whole space is much less strict or defined than it is in a larger office
with more specialization. In a four-person office, the browsing area
should "flow" into the sales area without any strong or definite division
and should encourage customers to come in. As the browsing and sales
area are included one within the other, the more specialized office
functions also included here in the general sales area are the typing or
clerical area, accounting, and so on. One separate office, which could be
used for private talks or conferences with clients or staff, supervision or
arrangements for special travels, is recommended. The supporting
functions such as mail delivery, brochure filing system, storage and
maintenance, can be kept within one larger room accessible from a
secondary or service entrance. The coffee area could also be included in
this type of service room, which would serve all the needs of the staff
or operation.

Case Study of Rosenbluth Travel Agency

A study of one company's office needs can be very helpful in giving
a general understanding of all that is involved in office layout, even
though specific needs always differ. The Rosenbluth Travel Agency is
the case study selected because the author was the architect for the job
and because it has received quite a bit of favorable publicity.

The Rosenbluth Agency does quite a volume in individual travel

TYPICAL LAYOUT OF A TRAVEL AGENCY WITH 4-5 EMPLOYEES

STREET
WALKWAY
RECEPTION - BROWING AREA
ENTRANCE
SALES AREA
ACCOUNTING
MAIL, FILES
COFFEE AREA
SERVICE ENTRANCE
TOILETS
PRIVATE OFFICE

ACCOUNTING
TYPING
TICKETING
FILES, STORAGE
SPECIAL SALES AREA
MAINTENANCE, CENTRAL BROCHURE
AIRLINES
GROUP TOURS
STAIRS
UTILITY

MEZZANINE

WALKWAY
BROWING AREA
GENERAL SALES AREA
SUPERVISOR
MAIL, STORAGE
SERVICE ENTRANCE
COFFEE AREA
ENTRANCE
STAIRS
TOILETS

4-5 AGENCY EXPANDED TO 8-10 VERTICALLY   FIRST FLOOR

CONFERENCE ROOM - RECEPTION AREA
AIRLINE TICK.
GROUP TOUR
TICKETING
FILES
STORAGE
STAIRS
SPECIAL SALES AREA
CENTRAL BROCHURE
SUPERVISOR
PRIVATE OFFICE
ACCOUNT.
TYPING
MAINTENANCE SECURITY
ENTRANCE
PRIVATE OFFICE
SERVICE ENTRANCE
BROWSING AREA
STORAGE, MAILROOM, ETC.
STAIRS
GENERAL SALES AREA
TOILETS
COFFEE AREA

4-5 AGENCY EXPANDED TO 15 HORIZONTALLY   FIRST FLOOR

SUGGESTED DESIGN FOR FRONT VIEW

SUGGESTED INTERIOR DESIGN FOR 4-5 AGENCY BROWSING AREA

SUGGESTED INTERIOR DESIGN FOR 4-5 AGENCY SALES AREA

arrangements, as well as in the wholesaling of package tours. They sell some of these package tours themselves in addition to other travel agencies who have their own lists of potential clients. The agency is divided into specialized travel areas, such as airline travel, steamship travel, Europe, Carribean, United States, Orient, and others. Previously located in an upper floor operation in center city Philadelphia, Rosenbluth's expanding business forced them to look for new office space because they were unable to obtain more space in their old location. At that time, they were engaged in roughly the same type of travel business as they are today: retail and wholesale.

Harold Rosenbluth and Eugene Block, partners in the firm, felt that they could increase their retail business if they were located on a ground floor office space in approximately the same center city location. They found an old townhouse which required drastic remodeling within a half a block of the old facility.

The Rosenbluth operation at that time was a 75-year-old organization and had developed an image of being a friendly, low pressure group with highly qualified, professional personnel. They were a large operation, employing in excess of 25 persons, with every possibility of that number increasing substantially in the near future. All these factors had to be incorporated in the design for their new facility.

It was decided early in the design phase that some kind of divider would have to separate the browsing area from the main sales force. There were two possibilities. The first was using a wall-to-wall counter; the other, having a difference in elevation between the two sections. The latter was favored and used.

Another consideration was to have a front entranceway that was noticeable and memorable. Also, it should be designed in such a way that people could detect it from a block away in case they forgot Rosenbluth's exact location. The client wanted the exterior to be designed so as to encourage people to come in and browse.

A metal canopy was created to demarcate the location. This can be seen from blocks away as there are no other canopies in the vicinity. A good bold sign carrying the firm name made of anodized aluminum with white plastic letters, lit from behind, was set between the two walls of the recessed entranceway. This treatment of the façade

33

distinguished Rosenbluth's from other offices in the area and afforded the opportunity for carrying certain treatments and textures from the outside to the inside. For example, a warm gray quarry tile floor with a Spanish motif was carried from the outside recessed area through the reception area. By removing the plaster, the original brick walls of the old townhouse were left exposed. A floor to ceiling window wall was installed and a semi-circular motif was etched on the glass to prevent people from walking through it. Dark bronze anodized aluminum, which conveys a rich, warm appearance, was used for the supports of the window wall. An easy-to-open door with the name of the agency repeated on it was installed. Warm, familiar materials, such as the exposed old brick, were used to encourage clients to stop in and browse around, hopefully to buy a cruise trip to somewhere. The idea was to bring the outside inside psychologically. People too!

The recessed space was created to function as an outside reception area. In this space a translucent kiosk, lit from the inside, was installed. There, colored posters of various cities and resorts can be displayed by day as well as by night. This exterior area also affords space for special noontime entertainment. The location is in a busy central business and shopping area so that there is much noontime traffic. Special entertainments have included belly-dancers, an imported English bobby to direct traffic, the giving away of fresh daffodils on the first day of spring and many other public relations activities which have embedded the name and location in people's minds.

Because the townhouse had more than one story, the browsing and reception area was located in a double height space. This space is kept uncluttered, completely open and separated from the department areas by a change to a higher level. The browsing area is enroute from outside to the stairs leading to the various travel departments. The display itself is part of the reception area décor. The space is large enough so that anyone may feel free to take brochures without asking any questions, but can ask questions of the receptionist if he has any. This serves to separate the browsers from the clients more serious about making definite arrangements, and does not take up any of the valuable time of the departmental specialist.

Departmental specialists are strung along the upper area. The receptionist directs incoming clients to the proper area. Each area is provided with shelves above the desk which hold reference material and brochures for the specific geographic area served. The ceiling has been lowered and this adds to a more subdued feeling of serious business. Mechanical equipment has been hidden in the new ceiling which is covered with acoustical tile.

Walls in the travel area were kept light to make this relatively narrow space seem as wide as possible. This is staggered with exposed brick which ties in with the exterior and reception area, as well as retaining some of the character of the old town house structure. Carpeting on the upper level helps absorb sound and is of a warm, yet neutral, gold color.

Because the space is relatively narrow, the color scheme was kept simple, with splashes of coral in the easily moveable stacking chairs. Free-standing files divide the right from the left side of the travel areas. Lighting is recessed in the ceiling. This allows for flexibility in future departmental spatial arrangements. The narrow corridor feeling in the travel department is broken up by the changing width half way down the building, due to the addition of the staircase which leads upstairs.

The partners are located in the rear of the facility and their spaces are enclosed with glass panels. This creates more cozy and luxurious spaces where private business can be conducted. At the same time, the glass partitions afford both a view of the street and the department specialists. This latent supervision helps to tie the office together psychologically.

Airline reservations and bookkeeping are located on the second floor near the top of the stairs, accessible to the travel departments, yet in quieter areas. Also on the upper floor is the wholesale operation. Here the tour operators carry on the entire wholesale business, completely divorced from the commercial, retail operation.

The conference area is on the second floor and looks down on the reception entrance area as well as the travel areas. It is used for special clients and staff meetings.

The mail room is highly important because of the great volume of mail which is received and sent out each day. It is conveniently and

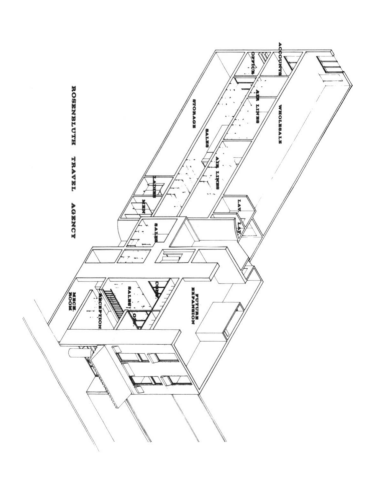

ROSENBLUTH TRAVEL AGENCY

unobtrusively located at the rear, where several secretaries divide the responsibility for its smooth functioning.

It can readily be seen that office layout is a prime factor in the functioning of a successful travel organization. At best, the layout can flexibly structure a creative, productive working environment, facilitating good client and employee relations. At worst, it can be an inflexible, cramped arrangement which freezes confusion. Flexibility is the key to good travel agency office layout. A layout must be able to adjust well to changes in the business. This is no small achievement. Competent professionals can help produce the kind of office layout which will function smoothly over a period of changes and time.

If professional help is sought in designing a travel agency, the results will be well worth the initial expense. An unworkable layout will cancel the most fervent employee enthusiasm. A monotonous, uniform facility, or one with chopped-up, unrelated spaces will cancel the most expensive public relations and promotional efforts. A good working plan will enable the agency, or new agency location, to function well and should be tailored to its particular space and office needs.

Chapter 3

Travel Agency Employees

by

Helen Hinkson Green

Smarter Recruiting Methods

Employee recruiting and selection is a process which can be a real key to improving productivity and office efficiency. In seeking the most beneficial methods of acquiring superior employees, a look at some ideals is a logical start. Study the following list to obtain a composite image of the ideal person for your organization. So doing will help to fix your pattern of procedure.

Ideally, your travel agency employee will be:
1. Mature enough to have good judgment.

2. Young enough in mind and heart to be eternally excited about the glamour and excitement of travel.

3. Empathetic enough to relate to all ages — and budgets — in customers.

4. Personally attractive enough to add class to the surroundings.

5. Extroverted enough that relating to people she works with comes naturally.

6. Cultured enough that correct English, good diction, and adequate vocabulary are just part of her.

7. Educated enough to know that Peru and Timbuktu are not exactly in the same corner of the world.

8. Good-natured enough to accept minor frustrations as a normal part of any day's expectations.

9. Curious enough that once she is "hooked" by the travel business she develops an insatiable thirst for learning more about all the fantastic places it is possible for people to go — via, naturally, the help of your agency.

10. Orderly and precise enough that *attention to details* is part of her pattern of living — not something that drives her distracted.

11. Traveled enough to know first hand both the fun of traveling and something of the planning that must go into well-executed vacations (even the casual kind), plus the realization that almost any vacation does not work out as planned *exactly*.

12. Handy enough with figures to readily spot an error caused by a misplaced decimal point or a date copied wrong.

13. Typist enough to produce tickets, reports, or whatever needs to be typed with reasonable speed, and can check them for absolute accuracy.

14. Penman enough that her handwriting is always legible to others — and herself.

15. Communication artist enough that her telephone conversation, as well as face to face contacts, get through with the meaning intended, both on the receiving and sending ends.

16. Organized enough to habitually "write it down" instead of trusting to her memory.

17. Team oriented enough to see herself as a part of the whole operation.

18. Cooperative enough to switch lunch hours, desks, or responsibilities without becoming upset or feeling pushed out shape about it.

19. Permanently attached to the community enough so that you can count on her staying with your organization indefinitely, provided the opportunities and incentives are in accord with her potential for service and growth.

20. Intelligent enough that, with a little practice, she can develop the ability to read other people's handwriting accurately.

21. Healthy enough that she is rarely ill enough to be away from the office.

22. Responsible enough to consider being at work important.

23. Self-disciplined and dependable enough that she can turn out the work despite innumerable distractions and interruptions.

24. Diplomat enough to be able to smooth ruffled feathers, pour oil on troubled waters, and head off minor confrontations among fellow workers without their even realizing that she has done so.

"Is that all?" you are probably gasping. "Dreamer! Let's get down to the real world. The one where such paragons don't exist. At least not

for what I can pay. Besides, just how would I test for such qualities? How would I know when I'd found such a gem?"

To answer your questions one at a time:

No, that probably isn't all. But that list will do for starters. To our knowledge there is no one test — nor even several tests — that will measure all of those qualities. But there are a number of things that you can do that will bring to light many of those qualities. We'll talk about them a little later. And you can't know for sure, until there's been a probationary period, just whether or not you've found such a one — nor even then for certain — but again there are things that can help you discern much. Until you have had the employee as a member of your team and provided proper orientation and given opportunities for growth and development, you may never come close to finding such an ideal employee, for a lot of those qualities and that expertise develop with orientation, supervision, training and opportunities you are willing to give. How ideal your employees become frequently depends upon ideal are the four things just mentioned.

A review and revision of your hiring, orientation and supervision practices may help you come closer to obtaining a reasonable facsimile of that ideal employee, granted that the real one rarely exists.

How Do You Hire?

Ask yourself some questions. Then ask yourself how your policies and practices might affect your business either favorably or adversely.

Do you hire her for how she looks? For what she can do? For both? Do you fit capacities and training to the job requirements? Or do you underhire or oversell the job?

Do you check references?

We hope your answer to that first three-part query was "both." But in all honesty do you sometimes let that first criterion obscure the second if she looks like a real swinger? Be honest.

We hope you said "yes" to the first part of the second major question up there, for either underhiring or overselling the job heads you for trouble. By underselling, we mean hiring a person who just doesn't have the requirements to do the job adequately or the potential to grow into it, largely because you presented the job requirements as being much simpler than they actually are; therefore both of you felt the individual was capable of handling a job that was beyond her capabilities.

By overselling, we mean building the job up (in the employment interview) so that it seems to contain more challenge and opportunity than it actually does possess, thereby attracting an individual capable of handling a much more demanding job and one with much more possibility for growth and advancement.

Either way, you are going to have a disgruntled, even unhappy, employee very shortly for reasons that neither of you fully comprehend. But the original *underhire* or *oversell* fault is the root of the trouble.

There is no excuse for anything but a "yes" answer to that final question. If you don't check references, you deserve what you get. You may argue that all references are given through rose-colored glasses; but any astute person can read between the lines, and a telephone call to the writer of a reference that you consider "less than glowing" may elicit much additional information that will help you make your decision. Teachers frequently bemoan the fact that businessmen never check with them to find out about the students they have trained. This state of affairs is all too often true. Protect both yourself and the prospective employee by carefully checking references.

Whom Do You Hire?

Again ask some questions. Again ask how your practices affect your business.

Do you hire –
The under 35 ones only?
The more mature ones? (chronologically, that is)
Full-time employees only?
Part-time ones for specific responsibilities?
Females only?
Some males?
High school graduates (or equivalent)?
College graduates?

If you say, "Well, I hire only the ones under 35 because they're more flexible, more open to innovation, and let's face it — more attractive," you won't get much argument, probably. Especially on that last point. But if turnover is one of your problems, had you thought about the fact that she is much more apt to quit, to have a baby or to move to another community because her up-and-coming young husband has been transferred, than is either her mother or grandmother — both of whom may also be in the available labor force? Older workers are inclined to stay put. Therefore, the age bracket in which you look for employees may have a definite bearing on the efficiency of your operation. So may others of those categories in that list. It might be wise, then, to apply two cautions to any criteria you have for hiring:

1. Do the advantages of employing such a criterion outweigh the disadvantages for my particular organization?

2. Am I making a mistake in *generalizing* too much about qualifications of people in this category?

44

Your Employment Interview

Of course you have one. Whether it is highly structured or extremely casual, its purpose is to help you assess the prospective employee's potential for fitting into your organization in a satisfactory and contributing manner. Its purpose should also be to help the prospective employee assess the job and you. The degree of structuredness may depend upon your opinion of what information you need to best assess the individual's potential for the job. If you require an involved application blank and several formal tests, your interview will take on a different character than if you keep things simple. It may or may not tell you more of what you need to know.

Obviously, the same sort of application blank and the same battery of tests that might be used in a very large organization with hundreds of office employees won't do the job for you. Possibly the reason many travel agency managers by-pass the use of an application blank is that they have tried (without careful adapting) some of the standard forms that just don't fit the needs of the position for which they were hiring. Quite frequently, some of these individuals do an excellent job of assessing qualifications and of hiring the right people as employees. Generally such agents aren't just lucky; they have resourcefully developed some very effective rule-of-thumb criteria that *work*. At least for them.

For example, one very successful agency manager shook his head smilingly when asked if he used an application blank in selecting employees.

"No," he said. "I can find out a lot more just talking to them. Oddly enough, I do have some very simple criteria that I apply that work for me. About four criteria, really. I'm not sure of why they really do help in finding the employees I'm after, although I have a sort of hunch for each of them. For any time I hire a girl who is short on any one of these four, she doesn't work out as well as someone who passes all four criteria. Yet they're so simple, I keep marveling that they have any discriminating power."

"Do you mind telling me what they are?" I asked.

"No," he said. "For what they are worth, here they are. But perhaps I should preface what I'm going to say by telling you that I really don't care whether a girl is a college graduate or even that she's had some college, although some would be nice. But if she measures up on the following things, I'll probably hire her, other things such as dress, speech, et cetera being acceptable.

First, she must have had a year of typing, or its equivalent. Everybody around here does some typing.

Second, she moves up a notch in my selection criteria if she has had two years of typing rather than just one. Now the funny thing about this is that she doesn't need typing *that much*, but I seem to get a different type of girl if she's had two years of typing instead of one. Perhaps it's that the girl with two years of typing will have taken more other business courses than the girl with just one year. Or perhaps it's that the two-year typist was more business oriented in the first place or she wouldn't have taken that second year. Or perhaps it's that in her second year of typing there were a lot of concommitant learnings that were a part of the typing course — working with various forms, making more decisions, planning her work, etc. Or perhaps it's knowing that she is a good typist gives her confidence in tackling not only typing but other tasks. Whatever it is, *two years of typing* measure for me more than just the difference in the ability to hit the keys.

Third, I ask her two very simple questions that tell me something primarily about her attitude — not necessarily her ability — to work with figures. It's the attitude that is important. I say, *"By the way, do you have a checking account?"* An affirmative answer tells me that she must rather like managing her own money, or having a say in the family money management if she's married. But my second question is the pay-off. I say, *"Do you balance your checkbook with your bank statement every month?"*

Invariably I get a reaction that tells me a lot — one way or the other. On the positive side are two reactions. She may say very matter of factly, "Of course." Almost as if I'd asked a very stupid question. Or she may even light up and say, "Oh, yes. It's rather

46

fun." On the negative side, she gives me a wry grin or throws up her hands with "Why bother? The bank is always right. Besides, it would drive me nuts hunting around for a few cents — or more likely a few dollars — to make it come out right."

Now an answer like either of the first two tells me invariably that I'm dealing with a girl who has a sort of natural ability to handle figures and that she also either does it so easily that she can't imagine not doing it or she really enjoys working with figures. Either way, she won't get all bogged down in the detail of figure work that is a part of the ticket business, or get it hopelessly messed up, or be continually bugged by having to do it. A girl who can't *stand* to handle a lot of detailed figure work, simple albeit but unendingly *there*, will never be happy or too effective in the spots I must place her. So such simple questions get me reactions that tell a lot.

My last question is *"Tell me a bit about yourself and your family. Do you ever take vacations trips of any kind?"*

Funny how revealing I've discovered that one to be. If she says, "Oh, indeed we do" and launches into an enthusiastic account of some trip, maybe just a weekend camping trip, I know she has a sort of feeling for travel — an awareness that any trip invariably has some unexpected developments — either bonus delights or minor disappointments — but she's a traveler at heart and accepts both kinds of developments as part of any vacation or trip.

But if she says something like, "No, we never could get away," or "We never had enough money," I know she may not have the same awareness of the first girl. There's a difference in the people who load everybody into the family car — broken down though it may be — and head for a state park on the Fourth of July and the people who think it's too much trouble, too expensive, or the car might break down. I'm not saying one type is better than the other. But they're different in their almost inherent feeling concerning what Travel is all about. And the girl who has grown up in a

47

vacation-taking family, simple though those vacations may have been, will fit into my agency better than the girl who has no vacation or travel mind or heart set — if there is such a term for it.

For what they are worth, you might begin applying those criteria in your own employment interviews — and adding simple ones of your own. Ask yourself, "What are the characteristics or qualities that my best employees have in common? Could I have discerned these qualities or characteristics in the initial employment interview by some simple questions or tests?"

An Application Blank that Tells and Tests

Illustrated on the following pages is an application blank that is very simple but effective and geared especially to the needs of travel agencies. It was developed for ASTS by Kielty-Rebedeau and Associates, State National Bank Plaza, Evanston, Illinois, and is reduced in size and reproduced here with permission of both ASTA and Kielty-Rebedeau and Associates.

Analyze it carefully. Each portion tells much, especially if you read between the lines. Couple it with those questions we just discussed and you may find that you do indeed have a simple but effective combined application form and testing program.

What about More Tests?

Some of you may be saying, "But if that combination or something equally simple doesn't do the job, what about more tests?" That's a question you'll have to answer for yourself. Certain tests do have the capacities to help fill in missing parts of the picture that gets partially filled in during an employment interview. But make no mistake. Do not think that tests are a substitute for the interview. Know, too, that unless tests are administered by trained personnel, their results can be incorrectly interrupted. Also realize that though many tests are valid in that they measure what they purport to measure, they just don't fit your particular situation or needs. A simple instrument, such as that ASTA "Application for Employment" form, which is also a very good testing device for your particular applicants, may do more to give you a complete picture of an applicant than a whole battery of tests. You are

48

APPLICATION FOR EMPLOYMENT
Please fill out this form in your own handwriting

To help us identify you among the other applicants ...

Name _____ Nickname _____ Marital Status _____

Address _____ Age _____ Previous Marriages _____

Town _____ Height _____ Ages of children _____

Phone _____ Weight _____ Social Security # _____

Pronunciation of your name _____ Driver's License # _____

To help us know you better as a person ...

What subjects did you enjoy most in school? _____

What subjects did you enjoy least? _____

What hobbies do you have? _____

_____ Why do you enjoy them? _____

_____

What kinds of job are held by other members of your family? _____

_____

What was the most boring or dullest part of any job you ever held? _____

_____

What was the most enjoyable part of any job you ever held? _____

_____

If you could begin to prepare for a career all over again, what would you most like to be?

_____ Why? _____

_____

What kinds of job are held by many of your close friends? _____

_____

What positions would you like to hold in any club or society? _____

_____

What positions would you enjoy least in any club or society? _____

_____

Where do these people live? Write your answers next to the pictures.

Which cultures do these famous scenes represent?

2

To help us learn about your experience . . .

Schools attended	Year entered	Year left	Gradu-ate?	Major Accomplishments

Military Services	Year entered	Starting rank	Year left	Final rank	Nature of Discharge
Draft Status			Reserve Status		

Previous Employers (in chronological order)	Dates Mo. & Yr.	Describe Duties	Union Affil.	Starting & Final Salary	Reasons for leaving
Name Address Supervisor	to			$____ to $____	
Name Address Supervisor	to			$____ to $____	
Name Address Supervisor	to			$____ to $____	
Name Address Supervisor	to			$____ to $____	

To help us learn your personal attributes as they pertain to this job . . .

STABILITY & RESPONSIBILITY

Have you ever been sued? (explain) _____

Do you have a police record? (explain) _____

How many traffic violations have you had in the last 5 years? _____ Types? _____

Are you in arrears on any financial obligations? _____ To what extent? $ _____

HEALTH

What confining illnesses have you had? (3 weeks or longer) _____

What chronic afflictions do you have? _____

What physical disabilities do you have? _____

How is your vision? _____ How is your hearing? _____

SOCIAL

How many intimate friends have you had for 5 years? _____ ; 10 years? _____ ; 15 years? _____

How frequently do you associate with your most intimate friends? _____

How long did it take to get well acquainted with most of your neighbors? _____

3

51

To help us evaluate your facility with arithmetic ...

The fare from city A to city B is ninety-five dollars and twenty cents.
The Federal tax on travel is 10%. There are no other charges.

Compute the charge to a customer for a one-way trip to city B from
city A. $_____

This customer wishes to continue his travels by visiting city C.
The fare from city B to C is thirty-eight dollars.

How much would his ticket cost for the complete journey? $_____

If this customer takes his wife, her fare is one-third less than his.
What would her fare be? $_____

When this customer arrives in city C, he and his wife will stay in a hotel room for 2 nights and
rent a car for use in his business. He will drive the car 138 miles before he returns it to the
hotel office of the rental agency. The room charge is sixteen dollars a day single and twenty
dollars a day double. The car will cost twelve dollars a day plus eleven cents a mile.

Our customer's company will pay only for his portion of the travel expenses.

He has asked us to compute all the charges so he can pay the total bill and also compute the
charges as if he had made the trip alone. Please do so.

Charges for combined trip	Charges for man only
Air fare _____	Air fare _____
Hotel _____	Hotel _____
Car rental _____	Car rental _____
Total _____	Total _____

To help us contact your personal references ...

List 3 personal references we may contact. Please do not include members of your family.

	Name	Address	Phone
1.	_____	_____	_____
2.	_____	_____	_____
3.	_____	_____	_____

I understand that any false statements or misrepresentations in this application will result in
severance of employment if already employed. Also, I authorize you to contact my references
and previous employers for additional information and release them from liability for damage
through furnishing this information.

Date _____   _____
                                                     Signature of applicant

much more likely to read between the lines correctly on a simple instrument than on a more complicated one.

But if you are looking for a performance test of clerical skills, in addition to those required on the blank, probably the best thing you can do is to give the applicant some sample jobs right out of the work crossing the desk which the applicant will "man" if hired.

If you are looking for some rule-of-thumb figures on the skill components alone, she is on the *top edge of average* if she can

type 50 words per minute accurately

take shorthand at 100 words a minute

transcribe 6 - 8 average length (150 words) letters an hour.

Two sources of information concerning tests are Purdue Research Foundation, Lafayette, Indiana 47901, and American Psychological Association, 1333 Sixteenth Street N. W., Washington, D. C. 20006.

Some of the tests that you might be interested in finding out a little about, just in case you do decide to give testing a try, are

SRA Verbal
Wonderlic Personnel Test
Thurston Mental Alertness
Thurston Temperament
General Clerical Test (Psyc. Corp.)
Blackstone Stenographic Proficiency Test
Kuder Preference Test
Remington Rand 5 minute typing test

What Do You Pay?

We can't talk about hiring and keeping good employees without talking about salaries and wages sooner or later. It might as well be right now in the form of two forthright questions.

Are your salaries competitive?

Can you afford noncompetitive salaries?

The answers to those two questions will tell you much about the caliber of the employees you may be able to obtain. Obviously, the more competitive your salaries, the better shape you are in. And, obviously, if your salaries aren't truly competitive, you have to look at that area of "Other Incentives" in which you may find you have some stellar attractions. There are incentives other than pay. Ask yourself honestly, "Why would someone rather work here than some place else?" The better answer you can come up with, the better chance you have of getting and holding the kind of employees you want.

Incentives for Holding and Developing Workers

Perhaps the best way to get at this topic is to tell you the story of an employee who wasn't being held. Remedy all the reasons why she was quitting her job in a travel agency and you might come up with a rather effective program of incentives. But let me tell you about it.

It was quite by accident — or was it? — that the girl at the first desk in the agency was the one who wasn't busy, and also quite by accident — or was it? — that she was giving notice of leaving that evening. She looked positively startled when I told her that I'd like to make appointments to talk to two people in the agency — the supervisor and the newest employee — provided the newest was also the most inexperienced insofar as the travel business was concerned.

"Well, I certainly qualify as the newest and most inexperienced," she said. Then reaching into her pocket she said, "But here is my notice that I'm leaving that I'm handing in at five o'clock tonight. It probably disqualifies me for whatever you want," she added with a weak little smile.

I hastily assured her that it most certainly didn't and that what she could tell me might be of great help to a lot of people. Being able to help seemed to appeal to her greatly, for her eyes brightened and she suggested that perhaps we could talk then and there since no one was coming in at the moment. So we did.

Rather quickly I learned that in addition to being most attractive, she was a college graduate with a major in Personnel Administration. She had also elected a course somewhere along the way in something or other about travel agency business just because she was interested in travel. "It was the most fascinating course I ever took," she said. "That's why at first I tried to get a job working in an agency. I got turned down by the one I wanted because I didn't have any experience. I don't blame them. I didn't. So I took something else."

She paused a moment. "Are you interested in all this?"

I assured her that I was, so she continued.

Learning by Experience

"Then my husband got a job in Guest City and we moved there. It just happened that when I applied for a job at the travel agency there, they had a vacancy in a one-girl branch. So, just like that, they hired me and sent me to work there."

"So you learned about the business fast?" I asked.

"Not really," she said. "I'd personally never put an inexperienced person in a one-employee situation like that with nobody to learn from. Later, when we moved back here, I applied again with this agency and was hired right in the main office. I was now *experienced* — but I really wasn't. Later they transferred me out here when they opened this branch."

Lack of Incentives

"It's such a beautiful office," I said, looking around at the modern décor, the beautiful colors, and exotic travel artifacts. "I can't imagine a more beautiful place to work."

"It is," she said. "I'll miss that. And I love this kind of work. I'd stay in a minute at the pay I'm getting if the incentives were here. But they aren't. And I can't stay without them."

"But isn't good pay one of the most tangible incentives?" I asked.

"Yes, it is," she said. "And the wage is adequate — at least for what I'm doing, I suppose — but it's the other things."

"What other things?" I asked. "It can't be the surroundings. And you're right at the first desk. Don't you get the first opportunity to make a sale if someone wanders in?"

Experience and Job Placement

"The first desk," she said rather sadly. "Do you know why I'm on the first desk? Because I'm the least experienced girl in the office. This is probably the spot in the office where the most time is wasted in nonprofit endeavor. It's the sort of buffer to absorb people who just

55

wander in with some idle questions about possible tours to someplace or other."

I winced a bit inwardly, thinking about the time I was taking up. But she had invited me to stay, and no one else had come in. So I nodded encouragingly.

"In a way, I can't blame them for putting me here. If you were running an agency, who would you put on the most unproductive spot? Your highest paid employee or your lowest one?"

"But doesn't being on the first desk give you the first chance at the new business that comes in? Aren't you all primarily sales people? And doesn't being on the first desk boost your sales record?"

She gave me a look of incredulity. "When I'm told, 'Don't sell any place you haven't been'?"

"And you haven't been many places?" I interrupted. "So you can't sell them?"

"Exactly," she said. "So I just have to say in essence, 'Look, I have to pass you along to someone smart enough to help you.' "

"Enough of that and you begin to feel du--, *incompetent*?" I asked.

"You were right the first time," she said. "*Dumb*. Slightly moronic."

"She's too intelligent for the performance level they've set for her, and too untrained and unknowledgeable for the level she could easily move to — with proper orientation and training and experience," I thought. But I kept my thoughts to myself.

"In a way, I can see their point about 'Don't sell where you haven't been.' " she said. "You're bound to make some mistakes when you don't know firsthand what the accommodations are like and what there is to see and do. You can certainly do a more creative selling job when you've actually been there. You see, selling really is a creative task — only you let the prospective customer do most of his own creation, really. You actually turn out to be the resource person. It's like the professor said in that course I took, 'Travel is a delightful business to be in because essentially, in so many instances, you are selling happiness. Or at least helping to create it through your efforts.' "

Her face had really lighted up as she spoke. "And they are letting that one get away!" I thought sadly. "What a waste of potential."

56

"And that's the sort of thing I mean when I say the incentives just aren't here for me," she went on. "I just can't live day after day feeling — being made to feel — inadequate about the whole situation. Not seeing opportunities for using my talents in that sort of creative way. And I do think I have some. Nor being trusted to develop any such creative abilities. Why I'm quitting is really between the job and me, really."

"What a perfect case she's building for the *hygiene factors-motivators* theory boys," I thought to myself. (And we're going to talk about them later on in this chapter.) "And she truly has psyched out her situation rather well."

"I'm taking up too much of your time," I said. "Perhaps I'd still better make that appointment." There was a lot I could still learn from her, I felt.

"As long as there is nobody coming, in *stay*," she said. "What else did you want to know?"

Skills and Employee Training Methods

"Two categories of things quickly," I replied. "First, just what office skills do you need to handle the work you do; and, second, if you were going to train whoever will replace you, do you have some suggestions as to how you would go about it?"

"Indeed I do," she said with a quick grin. "But do you want to get that first category out of the way first? It's really quite short. However, there are some real essentials."

"Such as?"

"Telephone ability and receptioning. Let's put it this way. The *ability to communicate* is the most essential skill needed, by far. And that means in all ways — face to face, phone, looks, nuances of expression — the ability to read them, that is. The ability to listen. That's a big part of communication. Excellent English, of course, good vocabulary, and a well-modulated voice. And a wide knowledge of geography and current world conditions and happenings is a part of the ability to communicate, when you come right down to it." (Later, I wondered why she hadn't mentioned the "ability to sell" over the telephone as one of the requirements for the job. Then I remembered her "don't sell any place you haven't been" remark and the ommission "figured" — at least in her case.)

"Typing?" I asked. "Do you need typing?"

"Some," she said, pointing to the ticket in her machine. "But as long as we're accurate, speed isn't imperative. The jobs are short. Like tickets, for example."

"Any other machines?"

"Very simple ones — at least in this office," she replied. "And for many offices these would probably be representative. How to use a ten-key adding machine, a postage meter, a photocopier. Actually, the so-called machine skills needed are minimal. The tools needed, actually, in addition to that ability to communicate, are *experience* and *proper* training."

"Then if you were going to train your replacement, how would you go about it?"

"Oh, I love this," she said, her eyes brightening. "For I do have some ideas."

"Such as — ?" I prompted again.

"*Such as putting the new employee at ease.* That's very important. There is so much to learn here that you can't know everything right at first. Make the employee aware of the fact that you are aware of this. And I'd go over and over, perhaps *where* you look for *what!* There are so many places that it takes some time for it all to sink in."

"Did you have some sort of a *Desk Manual* — a reference that tells you not only *what work flows over your desk*, but which also has a section on *References*, where to look for what, as you just said? And a section with *samples of the various forms* you use in doing the work, with correctly *filled-in illustrations* and key points noted, like 'Never forget to validate the ticket before you give it to the customer,' for example? And a section on — "

"Oh, I could have used *you*," she said. "You mean there really are such books? Books that describe not only what you do at a particular desk, but how — and what was it you said, 'the work flow'? What did you call it — a *desk manual*?"

"Yes, that's what I called it. And there really are such books, but only when somebody or other takes the time to prepare one for the

58

particular flow of work that crosses a particular desk — in your case the desk of the newest office worker."

"Just a well-organized section on *Where to look for what* — with some examples ranging from simple to tricky — would have been invaluable," she said.

"Good," I said. "Let's just pretend that such a DESK MANUAL is available to the new worker you're going to train and that you tell her to feel free to ask any questions concerning anything she finds therein. What then?"

I'd be very careful to establish proper rapport with her and to identify the channels of communication. I'd try very hard to make her feel that this is *our* office, that she will be an important part of it, and that it is important that she *enjoy* being a part of the team. If she isn't going to enjoy working here, she would be better off elsewhere and certainly the agency would be better off without her." She paused. Then she added with a quick little rueful smile, "I guess that sort of sums up why I'm leaving. You see, corny as this may sound — and sentimental — that bit about a travel agency's selling happiness largely is true. People come in to plan travels that represent maybe years of happy dreaming. They need to deal with individuals who can be empathetic with such dreams. A disgruntled employee isn't going to be able to help them as they deserve to be helped."

"It doesn't sound corny to me," I assured her. "But it does represent a new concept to me. One that makes eminent sense. But go on, please. What next?"

Conducting Training Sessions

"Next I'd have some real training sessions — some simulated selling experiences, which I'd set up with the new employee and me (her trainer) seated at a long table in the back room — a table big enough to hold all sorts of references that we might need. And I'd do these first sessions in the back room, so she wouldn't be embarrassed before she had a chance to know everything. Later, we could move out and have more advanced sessions with her sitting beside my desk." It was almost as if she had anticipated my question about that back room that I was about to ask.

"First, I'd explain the references and point out how certain things in them can be found quickly by referring to that *reference section* she's going to have in that desk manual somebody is going to have ready for her," she said with a grin. (The grin almost surely designated me to do it.) "Like where to find something in this OAG that comes out every month — both the domestic and the international one."

I nodded in agreement, so she continued.

"Then I'd suggest that she do some reading in the materials, write down certain key points and questions, sort of like homework. It really is homework. Then we'd have another session with review of the simple things. Then we'd work up progressively to more difficult things." She paused a moment, then continued.

"Then I'd give her some practical examples. Sometimes I'd have her play the role of the customer and I'd look up the information and figure the fare, etc. Sometimes we'd reverse the roles. We'd continue this phase of the training until she felt secure about handling some of our fictitious situations. How long would depend upon the individual, of course. Some would learn more quickly than others, naturally. Two weeks would probably be ample time for most trainees."

"What else?" I prodded.

Airline Ticketing Seminars

"Oh, then, I'd let her attend one of the seminars on ticketing that the various airlines hold — just as soon as possible. You really do learn from these. They're wonderful."

"How long are these seminars?" I asked.

"They vary. Sometimes two days. Sometimes an afternoon. Even longer, if you go to ticketing school."

"Anything else?"

"Well, it would help if she could travel some right away. I can see reasons why the new employees aren't eligible for expense-paid trips — but, oh, how it would help a new employee if she could travel right off."

"I can agree with you on both counts," I told you. "But feasible or not, maybe we can start a *hold-the-thought*, two-woman campaign for such." And we grinned at each other. "Stranger things have happened. Who knows?"

60

Creative Client Selling

She nodded. "It certainly would help if ever it could happen. But all these suggestions have been quite structured. And I think they should be, in the beginning. But once she begins to feel comfortable, I'd let her feel free to work out things on her own. After all, as I keep saying, selling of any kind is creative — and selling travel is definitely so. The employee's attitude toward each customer and his travel wishes are as important a part of her success as anything. Does she sense (or find out) what it is the customer is really wanting to buy? A ticket, of course. But along with that ticket what does the customer really hope he is purchasing? A lot of hopes and dreams are frequently tied up in tickets. Or ambitions and projects. Or business successes and failures. Perhaps, if the ticket isn't right, other things don't go right either."

Importance of Incentives

That wasn't quite all of what she told me, but if you go back and read between the lines carefully, you have a rather clear picture of why employees sometimes quit, even though the pay is adequate, the surroundings beautiful and the fellow workers pleasant. What incentives were missing?

The Incentives — Other than Pay

Anyone who knows much about the travel business knows that there are relatively low ceilings upon what an agency or bureau can pay, initially and ultimately, to an employee. To stay competitive, then, and to hold good employees, you have to look at *incentives* — other than pay — that can attract and hold an employee. Let's look again at the situation of the girl who was quitting for some clues. These things, normally thought of as incentives, were there:

The pay, while not the best, was adequate. "The pay is all right if the other incentives were here," she said.

The surroundings were absolutely beautiful.

The immediate supervisor was "just terrific."

The other employees were nice to work with.

In addition, there were these *plus qualities* going for her on the job.

She had the right mental attitude. She really "dug" the travel business. Almost any agency manager would applaud her feeling that the real business of the agency is selling, and the perceptive ones would certainly go along with her attitude toward the basic nature of the commodity sold.

She had a certain amount of training, whether she thought she did or not. There was that elective course she had taken in travel agency business and she had worked in the one-girl branch office.

She was a college graduate with a major in personnel management.

She certainly had looks, intelligence, a better-than-average vocabulary, and an exceptional ability to communicate.

So what was wrong? Certainly it was an "Employee Job Satisfaction Problem" if you ever saw one. And you can't dismiss it with saying, "Well, I'd like to hear the supervisor's side of the story. There are always two sides to any problem situation involving people." We'll grant the last observation readily. But without going into it, let's accept the situation as being as the girl *perceived* it to be. For to her it *was* as she perceived it, regardless of how you or I or her supervisor may have perceived it. If we could just accept that fact and govern our actions accordingly, we could probably improve employee satisfaction to a higher degree and much more often than we routinely do.

Job Satisfaction in the Work Itself

A quick run down on some of the theories and concepts that have to do with job satisfaction and problems might help us come up with insights and guidelines. Actually, a number of the theories or concepts saw little, if any, relationship between the quality of job satisfaction and the qualities inherent in the work itself. Later theorists began to believe that there was a definite relationship between the nature of man and the nature of the work he did that had great bearing upon this thing called job satisfaction. This concept knocked some of the older theories right out of the ball park.

Just to refresh your memory, a review might look like this:

The Protestant ethic
The economic man
Scientific management and work simplification
The instrumental man

62

The dissatisfiers and the satisfiers (single continuum theory)
The hygiene factors and the motivators (dual continuum theory)

Without going into a review of all the ones that didn't work too well or even hold up in theory, let's examine that last one. And as a necessary prologue to it, let's take a quick look at that single continuum theory. You might be interested in getting a fuller picture by reading *Work and the Nature of Man*, by Frederick Herzberg, published by the World Publishing Company, New York, 1966.

The single continuum theory was based upon the premise that man's life consists in part in his being in "equilibrium" with his environment. Anything that upsets that equilibrium is a dissatisfier and therefore reduces his satisfaction with his environment — the status quo — his job satisfaction to bring it down to cases in one area of his life. So the more pleasant you make the working conditions, the more satisfactions you pile in or on (by removing dissatisfiers), the more job satisfaction he will have. Don't leave him anything to be dissatisfied about. Give him air-conditioning, fringe benefits, such as hospitalization, insurance of all kinds, sick leaves, longer paid vacations, shorter hours, new glasses, new teeth, et cetera, plus, of course higher pay; and just watch that dissatisfied worker turn into a satisfied one.

It sounds good, and no one will deny that it works — up to a certain point. After a while, you reach a point of diminishing returns. After a surfeit of good working conditions, fringe benefits, higher pay, he is dissatisfied again. "Oh, if you have to work for a company, EezyBreezy Company is O. K. or even among the best, but — " And he can give you all sorts of reasons why working for any company is a lousy way of life. Why?

According to Herzberg and others, the fallacy lies in thinking that dissatisfiers and satisfiers lie along a single continuum, that they are simply varying degrees of the same thing. The single continuum theory also accepts, ever so subtly, one facet of the Protestant ethic — the prong that states that man is condemned to work; therefore work is an onus, something to be borne. So make it as palatable as possible; *ergo*, reduce the dissatisfiers. Up go the satisfiers.

The dual continuum theory discounts both of these premises. First of all, it is predicated upon the idea that man really enjoys work that challenges him, that gives him a chance to prove his ability to wrestle with problems and to solve them, and that gives him an opportunity to excel in his work. Furthermore, it rejects the idea that dissatisfiers and satisfiers are more or less of the same thing, holding rather that they are from different bases, proceed on different strata or continuums. Improving the working conditions in order to improve a man's job satisfaction is like trying to satisfy a man's need for air by giving him water. Air and water are not more or less of the same thing. Neither are satisfiers and dissatisfiers.

Hygiene Factors and Job Motivators

According to Herzberg (see previous reference, *Work and the Nature of Man*), the hygiene factors (so-called because of their resemblance to the hygiene factors in medicine) and the motivators represent the two continuums in the dual continuum theory. Just as you don't cure or remove a malignant growth from an individual by giving him pure drinking water, a clean bed, fresh air, and excellent nursing care, neither do you cure or remove whatever is inherently wrong with the work itself by improving the working conditions. The motivators are *not* just an absence of dissatisfiers. Look at the two lists below:

Hygiene factors	*Motivators*
Company policy and the administration	Achievement
Supervision	Recognition
Interpersonal relations	Status
Working conditions	Personal dignity
Salary	Acceptance by peers

The group on the left are concerned primarily with the enviromental conditions affecting the work; the group on the right, with conditions or qualities arising out of the work itself. The motivators bear a striking similarity to the basic psychological needs of man: *a positive self attitude, recognition, status, personal dignity*, and *acceptance by peers*.

You can argue, and rightly so, that improvement of the working conditions, better pay, and fringe benefits influence some of the things listed both as motivators and as psychological needs of man. They do indeed, to a degree. But only to the extent that those components considered to be satisfiers are fulfilled through the work itself will you probably have the kind of incentives in a job that would *hold* the girl who was leaving, a girl who had tremendous potential to be an outstanding employee.

For example, an opportunity to sell, even though she hadn't been to the places sold, or, better yet, a bit of recognition for some small creative suggestion might have worked wonders for her deflated self-image.

If you would find and *hold* excellent employees, despite all competition, look for the motivators — the job enrichment possibilities for your employees. Don't mistake job enrichment for mere job enlargement. And don't confuse motivators with the hygiene factors. Don't toss out the hygiene factors as being unimportant. They play a part. But the real motivators are inherent in the work itself.

Placing the girl just described in a position of more responsibility so that she could achieve more would have given her some of the "inherent in the work" motivators. The choice of a new position for her would be based upon the criteria of achievement, recognition, and status. Incidentally, both her status symbol and her self-concept might be greatly enhanced by a change in title to say, "travel counselor."

Orientation and Supervision

How good are your orientation and supervision practices? The girl who was quitting gave us not only some practical suggestions for such practices but some hints of how important such practices were, didn't she? No employer or organization can afford to ignore the problems of adaptation that a new employee faces nor the pressures that he feels are exerted upon him. (Remember how many times that girl used the word *threatened*?) Without proper orientation and supervision a potentially good employee may resign; a mediocre or poor one will sour or barely hang on.

Job orientation is basically an effort to allay the anxieties a new employee may feel about unfamiliar environment and tasks. New workers must be given time to cope with the difficulties of adjustment and of learning. First impressions must be pleasant. A worker usually spends as much time in an office as he spends with his family. That is a lot of time when you think about it. Negative first impressions, no matter how unreasonable or illogical, could cause irreversible damage in attitudes and feelings.

In his *Work and the Nature of Man*, Herzberg cites a line from the play "Death of a Salesman" that could apply to all employees. It is that poignant line uttered by Willy Loman's wife in speaking through her grief and remorse after the demise of Willy: *"Attention must be paid!"* An employee's work life may be at stake if attention is not paid. He just won't be there!

Poor Willy messed up his life and died. Employees, sensing that they are messing up theirs, may just quit and start over some place else before too great psychological harm has been done.

Self-test Concerning Orientation and Supervision

If you can answer each of the following questions in the affirmative, you are probably doing a good job of orientation and supervision. If you find negative answers cropping up, perhaps you had better review and revamp your orientation and supervisory policies and practices.

1. Do you have an initial training period?

2. Are there tours or trips that new employees may take that will help them become familiar with both travel and places? (Could this one come true, somehow?)

3. Are there manuals, other than the tariff manuals, the hotel directories, etc., that describe exactly the work procedures for a given "desk"?

4. Are the duties well defined?

5. Are work priorities set up?

6. Are the lines of authority clear?

7. Are the agency policies clearly spelled out?

8. Were the job possibilities and the pay incentives clearly spelled out in the employment interview?

9. Does the employee feel that someone is concerned about her advancement and pay raises? Or, if there is little opportunity for either, was this spelled out in the initial interview?

10. Do you avoid the following all-too-common faults of supervision?

    Hover and smother
    ignore
    delegate responsibility to someone ineffective as a supervisor

11. Do you give recognition for work well done?

12. Do you provide opportunity for initiative?

13. Do you delegate tasks after proper training?

14. Do you provide opportunity to learn more about the many facets of the job?

15. Do you see that the relevance and relationships of what the employee does to the total operation is understood?

16. Are you alert to signs of "square pegs in round holes" regarding the type of work?

    (Remember that question about "Who balances your checkbook?" That simple routine might help eliminate a square peg before she got started.)

17. Do you listen and attend to grievances?

    (Listening and attending to grievances takes cognizance of that admonition that "Attention must be paid.")

18. Do you ask your employees for suggestions — and give the suggestions thoughtful consideration?

19. Do you honestly think that your employees feel that they are a part of a team?

20. Do you honestly think that your employees consider you a good supervisor?

How did you do? If you want to live courageously, why don't you duplicate the list and have your employees rate you? Anonymously, naturally. (Just because you decide to live courageously is no reason for them to live dangerously. Right?) A comparison of the two sets of ratio might be revealing of how differently individuals perceive the same situations, to put it nicely. It could result in some improved orientation and supervision practices, too.

The ASTA Correspondence Course as a Training Tool

Undoubtedly you know about the ASTA correspondence course for those interested in travel agency work. But do you use it as an instrument for upgrading both prospective employees and the presently employed ones? Including yourself? It is worth considering for both groups if you don't already make use of it.

Granted that such a practice might put a strain on the "Orientation and Training Budget" (we won't ask for a show of hands of how many have one) to purchase courses for each employee, but it might pay off in the long run, at that. Perhaps you could chalk it up as a fringe benefit or a donation to education, or something that you could write off for tax purposes. (I'm joking about that — or am I?) At any rate, if you want well-trained employees, look into the possibility of that

ASTA correspondence course. You might even do as some companies do about night school tuition for their employees. Reimburse an employee, at least partially, upon successful completion of the course. Lest there be any misunderstanding about my waving such a fervent flag for the course, let me hasten to say that I get no commission from ASTA. I just think you are passing up a good thing if you don't make the best possible use of it. The eventual achievement of the CTC (Certified Travel Counselor) designation, established through the institute of Certified travel agents for your management employees is also a commendable program.

Exit-interview Information as a Source of Upgrading Practices

The big hang-up in exit interviews is that the person quitting doesn't often come through with the real reasons for leaving. Either he is too polite or thinks, "Why bother?" since obviously it's too late to do him any good. But perhaps the sort of information you hope to glean from an exit interview could be secured from a follow-up letter and brief questionnaire mailed to the individual almost immediately after he has left your employment. Tell him in the letter, which is genuinely courteous, that you are asking for help in your efforts to improve your agency's policies in orientation, training and supervision, and work organization. You might get some straightforward and revealing answers.

With the help of your employees, dream up your own little "Exit Review of the Situation at XYZ Agency." After you have secured the essential personal data at the top of the form, ask the same sort of question you might ask in an exit interview if you weren't substituting this questionnaire follow-up procedure for it. Questions such as —

What did you like most about your job?
What did you like least about it?
What was your biggest frustration in connection with your job?

What did you like most about the agency?
What did you like least about the agency?
Were you satisfied with the training you received?

Did you feel competent to do the work required of you? If "Yes," explain briefly. If "No," explain briefly.

What suggestions do you have for improving training for new employees?

Why did you leave our employment?

Would you ever want to work for the agency again, provided conditions remained essentially the same?

Would you ever want to work for the agency again, provided certain conditions changed? If you said "Yes" to this question, please cite briefly what changes you would wish to see.

You may not like all of the answers, but if you are seriously interested in getting and keeping good employees, the opinions of those who leave your employ may be of considerable value to both you and your present and future employees. Provided, of course, you interpret them in the light of how the findings can help you improve your employment practices.

Chapter 4

Organizing the Work

by

Helen Hinkson Green

The organization pattern of any size travel agency will vitally affect its efficiency and profitability.

How should the work be organized in your agency? The correct answer to that question is the same old one that earns a "B" in any course — "It depends upon the *climate* and the *terrain*." For just translate *climate* and *terrain* into the parameters of the particular situation you are talking about and you come up with a much better solution to your problem than you would obtain by following some hard and fast rules or dictums.

There is no *one* way to organize the work in your various offices for the reason that the number of employees you have, the hours and days you stay open, whether or not most of your business comes to you or you go after it, whether you hit the same peak and low seasons and at the same yearly times that others do, the varying abilities of your staff, their varying salaries, the availability of competent part-time help, and even the physical layout of your office — all have a bearing upon how the work should be divided. Oh, yes, add another important factor that should be taken into consideration in how you organize the work in your particular office — upon what do you base your pay increases and promotions? If, for example, you base these solely, or even largely, on the amount an employee *sells*, then in all fairness you have to organize the work so that every employee has equal time and opportunity to sell. You can't assign Susie to an hour on routine correspondence if in essence this is depriving her of an hour when she is potentially free to sell.

It truly is a question of climate and terrain, isn't it? The organization most efficient and effective for one agency will need modifications to be equally so in another. Therefore, don't expect a neat "This is the way you do it, folks" package or pattern in the next few pages. Rather, let's look at some guidelines and practices that you can bend to fit your particular work situation. Think about each of the following suggestions in line with your own organization. You won't like all of them, some of them certainly won't work in your particular situation — though they do in some other office. Some of them you already utilize effectively, but there just may be one or two that could make a difference *for the good* if you adapted them and tried them out. The old maxim, "It's the little things that make the big difference," holds in work organization. Please read with that attitude of mind. Now for the suggestions:

Personnel Utilization

Don't utilize high-salaried personnel on routine jobs that a lower-salaried person could do. If your best sales person spends as much time on filing brochures as your lowest-paid one, for example, it could be that you are paying too much for the filing. Many offices run up costs needlessly because the work performed is not fitted to the caliber of the employee or *matched* to his salary. How often have you walked into an organization or institution and noted a high-level secretary doing very routine work that an assistant stenographer or clerical worker could have done just as effectively? Or, even worse, the executive above the secretary doing tasks that should have been turned over to her. It's a vicious chain. Frequently the explanation given is that "We can't afford to hire anybody else." The truth of the matter, cost-wise, probably lies in "You can't afford not to." It might pay big dividends to analyze the work and reorganize it so that certain low-level or routine tasks could be handed over to a part-time employee. That leads right into the next suggestion.

Part-Time Employees Help

Consider the possibility of part-time employees – both on a regular basis and for peak or vacation periods. "Those aren't always easy to come by," you say. No – but often easier than you think. And sometimes the employment of part-time help is one of the best ways to get your work organized along functional lines, at least partially, as well as to cut costs. For example, consider having more of your book work handled by a local Certified Public Accountant or even an individual not so classified but who is an experienced accountant. It will probably represent a real economy in the long run, for with such professional help you will probably be able to know from month to month – or even day to day – your exact financial condition. If your agency's revenue reaches $100,000, you may be at the point at which the utilization of a data processing service may save you time and money as well as provide you with daily records of your financial condition. Knowing the shape you are in financially is essential to any long-range planning or work reorganization if it is to be done intelligently. If you don't know until the end of the year or tax time, you may be in for some unpleasant surprises.

Another area for part-time help is certainly the *filing*. "But the filing has to be done every day," you say. "You get behind on those tariff sheets and you're in trouble. You'd need that part-time help every day."

That's right. And such part-time help is quite likely to be readily available if you just look for it. You may not even have to look. Consider a work-station for the Co-op program for clerical practice that the local high school or community college runs as part of its office training program. Or if the work-station idea doesn't appeal to you, how about a business student to come in for an hour or two after school, or a young married woman who only wants to work a few hours each week? Again, this helps you organize at least certain areas of your work along functional lines. Certainly it would get the filing done at a cost below what filing is costing you when your most highly paid employees spend a part of their time doing it.

Still another area for part-time employees is during the rush before a big tour takes off. Here you may be able to utilize a former employee who is an old hand at handling such details. She might even do the work at home if coming in is a problem.

Those former employees can be tapped, too, for filling in on those extra Saturday afternoon or night hours when inexperienced part-time help won't do. Unless you get somebody to relieve the regular staff from those extra assignments, some of them have to take too many "turns" if not everybody knows how to "do everything."

Organize Work by Function

Decide how far you can go toward organizing the work by function. That last sentence in the preceding paragraph brings us to a consideration of whether you divide your work according to function or according to employee. If the agency is quite small, you may find your most efficient pattern of work is for everybody to be able to do everything — except possibly those tasks you farm out. Otherwise, when even one person is absent, the wheels of progress may grind to a slow pace if not a downright halt. Even in a larger office, it is well to have at least several people who are trained to do *everything*. Then if that part-time *experienced* help isn't available, not everybody has to come in for those extra odd hours — or work overtime if there is a rush. Also, if only one person, say, can handle everything, that one person really has to take the brunt of working at those times when a skeleton crew is needed. Therefore, no matter what the office management texts may tell you about the increase in efficiency and the corresponding reduction in cost, you will probably find that organizing the work along functional lines works only to a degree in your particular situation.

After you decide just how many of your people are going to need to be trained "or grow into" being able to do everything, examine each *function* and decide just what part can be given over to one individual

74

(or department in a larger office), and which parts of each transaction should be carried through by the individual with whom the transaction started. Look over the tasks that are susceptible to being handled as functions:

Receptioning (counter or desk)

Telephone (incoming calls)

Procuring and giving information

Selling travel

Writing tickets

Figuring tariffs and fares

Recording the money transaction (which may be handled in several ways)

Validating the tickets

Making up itineraries

Handling the incoming mail

Handling the correspondence

Paying the bills

Keeping track of equipment and supplies repairs and reordering

Doing the accounting work — several subdivisions are possible

Doing the banking

Handling personnel matters — hiring, training, supervision, work scheduling, raises, vacations, etc.

Managing the office

Ask yourself these questions:

1. How is each of these areas of work handled in our agency?

2. How many people are performing similar tasks or routines?

3. Is the pay scale for each of those on similar tasks commensurate with the performance level of the task?

4. At what point could the higher paid individuals be relieved of certain routine duties?

5. In which areas could work be delegated according to function?

6. Would increased efficiency result if such work were delegated according to function?

7. What effect would such reorganization have upon the rapport and morale of our office force? Upon clientele?

8. What suggestions do the employees have for reorganizing the work?

9. Do we really know how each employee utilizes her time?

If you don't readily know the answers to all those questions, perhaps it is time to find out — or at least try.

Enlist All the Staff

Get the cooperation of your entire staff in carrying out a work analysis and improvement program. You won't get to first base without it so don't start snooping around clipboard in hand *a la* good ole Charlie Brown in *Peanuts*, playing the big executive, until the staff is with you on the venture. (Remember Charlie's famous line when his ball team wasn't doing so hot, "I ought to be a good manager. I've even got a clipboard"?) It is going to take more than a clipboard to get you launched on this one. But with the support of your staff, a good self-study program will be worth it. One thing is certain. *There must be something in it for them.* The employees who will do a good job of it just for the glory of good old Zippy Zodiac Tours Bureau are few and far between — and they should be. Remember those hygiene factors and the motivators when you are outlining why and how such a program will be beneficial to all. A little of the first and a lot of the latter might really get you cooperation. With the cooperation assured, you can go ahead with the rest of the suggestions given in this chapter.

Rely on Staff's Know How

Ask for suggestions and be receptive to them. The people who do the actual work are certainly the ones most likely to come up with good suggestions for improvement. But they won't come up with a second or third one if you stop them cold with, "That's a good idea, but — " Or, "We tried that before you came and it doesn't work." Or, "We'll think about it and let you know." Being receptive means being willing to explore the suggestion with them. Chances are, if the suggestion is a dud, that the employee will be the first one to suggest scrapping it or to come up with feasible adaptations of it after such an exploration. Be sure to give credit where credit is due — in both tangible and intangible ways.

Think Time

Become TIME-CONSCIOUS and analyze how time is spent. You can't make time or enlarge upon it, but you can SAVE time. Even a very few minutes saved here and there adds up to a usable amount in a day, a noticeable amount over a period of a week, and a sizable amount (in terms of dollars and cents, too) over a month or a year. Take up the slack.

Someone has said that "Every fifth person in any office should be fired," meaning that even the best of offices operate at no more than

80 per cent efficiency. Incidentally 50 to 66 per cent is more nearly the normal ratio. So there is certainly room for improvement. But don't go around quoting that "Every fifth person" quote to your staff, or cooperation may drop to an all-time low. It does point up the fact that we should do a better job of coming to grips with time and work measurement in our office operations.

Although some M. T. M. studies (Methods Time Measurement) have been carried out and data compiled, it is difficult to get measurements on each operation, and even more difficult on each component of each operation that goes on in your office. In case you get interested in pursuing the work measurement bit in greater depth, back in 1947, Paul B. Mulligan became interested in office work measurement and his four-inch thick *Manual of Standard Time Data for the Office* gives time-values for some 5,000 office operations from making a key stroke on a typewriter to operating some of the latest equipment. (He didn't quit in 1947, in case you're wondering just how "late" 1947 equipment would be.) There were some other M.T.M. analyses that you might look into also. The Serge A. Birn Company's *Master Clerical Data System* observed and assigned time values to such body motions as standing, sitting, walking, reaching, putting down, etc. Booz, Allen & Hamilton Methods Service uses predetermined times for clerical operations as part of a system developed from motion-time measurement. Then there is the random sampling technique wherein an analyst (*time* analyst, that is, not the head-shrinking variety) walks through an office quickly noting what the various workers are doing or not doing. Repeating this procedure at random intervals, he arrives at an estimate of the rate of production to unproductive time. The big hitch in that method is that it reveals only if time is being wasted and if so, how much; but it doesn't get at how or by whom.

We aren't suggesting that you page all through the four-inches-thick Mulligan's *Manual*, or purchase Birn's Master Clerical Data card (a 6 x 9 inch affair by which a trained supervisor was supposed to be able to judge whether or not his staff was turning out the amount of work it should or whether any particular worker was working as well as she should), or that you hire an analyst to walk through periodically. You'll be about as popular as a hijacker with a time bomb would be among one of your tours if you do. But we are suggesting that you do take seriously this business of becoming TIME CONSCIOUS and analyze to the best of your ability how TIME is spent in your office and how savings in time can be effected — and how time spent can be spent more effectively. You might enlist each employee, including yourself, to check up on how he spends his time in one of the following ways:

(a) Keep time checks — say every ten minutes for a day or two. In simplest form, simply jot down what the individual is doing at each ten-minute interval. No form is required, just a blank piece of paper. Oh, yes, it is time consuming and tedious, but nobody is going to do it forever. Just for a day or two. And it is one of the best ways to spot *interruptions* to flow or completion of work. For example, on one time-check sheet we once analyzed, a girl who was typing a two-page stencil at 9:30 was still on the stencil at 11:30. But her time-check sheet showed why. She was working in a small office where many people came in with questions. Nobody thought she had many receptionist duties until they saw that time-check sheet. If the so-called interruptions turn out to be the primary work the individual should be doing — as in the case cited they were, priority should be given to them and the work reorganized and certain tasks allocated elsewhere.

(b) Another system is the Daily Log in which you block out the time in stated intervals. Block the time out in hours or half hours on a form you can quickly draw up that looks something like the illustration. You can make up your own.

TIME LOG FOR _Mary Smith_ Date _June 4_

Time	Activity	With Whom	What Accomplished
8:00	Phone- info on flight to Chicago	Self and Customer	Booked flight for three
8:30	Counter- inquiry on Hawaiian Tours	Self and prospective Client	Gave brochure and alternate fares and plans
9:00	Phone- info NY flights	Self and Customer	No booking

(c) A third similar version is the Start-Stop Log. This time you change that first column to record the time you start an activity and the time you complete it. This one gets a better look at what actually happens to time for people who have uneven work loads.

Start / Stop	Activity	With Whom	What Accomplished
8:30 / 9:10	Discussing proposed trip to Hawaii	Dr & Mrs a.C. Jones	Preliminary planning for possible trip

This is also a beautiful one for analyzing just how much time is spent in making a "sale." If you really want to get into cost analysis sometime, figure up the cost in *time spent* on a given sale before you start figuring the profit on the sale. You may not be making as much as you thought you were. Again, you may be making more. The point is — do you *know*?

(d) Still another method is the *guesstimate* technique. (No, I'm not being funny, and I didn't make it up.) This one is far less time-consuming, but also far less accurate. The employee in planning his day jots down the activities and after each his estimate (guesstimate) of the time it will take. As he finishes each activity, he writes the actual time it did take beside the guesstimate. Its biggest drewbacks are that it doesn't show all the things that we might have accomplished concommitantly with a task written down and many little flurries of activities that do get accomplished just before noon, perhaps, never do get accounted for.

But by some manner, try to get a picture of how each employee spends his day. Then as a second step, roughly analyze the time breakdown by some simple pie chart graphs. These will give an effective picture of what percentage of each person's time is spent in what. These pie charts are a good way of getting at that problem of discerning whether a high-salaried employee is spending too much time on routine jobs some one else could do.

80

And just the fact that everybody has become time-*conscious* helps to tighten up that slack time surprisingly.

You can get the habit of thinking about various phases of the work of the office along PERT lines, especially the multi-stage projects such as most of your big tours are. "But don't you need a computer for PERT? Wasn't the PERT technique designed by the Navy along about 1958 to guide its gigantic Polaris missile program to an early climax? What was it that PERT stood for? *Program Evaluation and Review Technique?*" That's right — on all counts. But notice we didn't suggest that you write PERT programs. We said you could get the habit of *thinking along PERT lines.* And you can.

Simply take the idea or basic plan of Program Evaluation and Review Techniques and apply a simple formula adapted to your own work, and you should come up with an evaluation and review that will sharpen your control of work organization and time control in a hurry. It's worth a try on some of your big projects.

Here's how you could determine a PERT time estimate. You analyze each component of the big task — guesstimate — in the following time components: (1) the *optimistic time* — if everything works out smoothly; (b) the *pessimistic time* — if everything possible that could go wrong should go wrong; and (c) the *most-likely time* — just what it says — the figure that most clearly represents what is realistic to expect for the accomplishment. Then you put the three times into a formula that looks like this:

$$\text{EXPECTED TIME} = \frac{\text{Optimistic} + 4(\text{Most likely}) + \text{Pessimistic}}{6}$$

You can link the various components into a simple flow chart type of diagram and there you are with a very realistic picture of the time the big project will probably take. You can even get fancy and use circles to represent the *events* and arrows to join them with the arrows symbolizing the *activities* (work) of the person or group of persons leading up to the events. Of course, in "perting" each component, you'll need to consult with the individuals who will actually be doing the work in each step involved. And therein will probably lie the greatest value in your *thinking* PERT. Your PERT network or plan can become a communications and teamwork vehicle.

Follow the Work

Trace the flow of various pieces of paper. Such a simple procedure can often point the way to more effective organization of the work in an office. Yours, perhaps. Why not give it a try?

Where was the paper first handled? What happened to it at this point of initial entry or initiation? Where does it go next? And next? And next — ? How many copies? What happens to each? How many people handle the paper? If more than one, how far apart are their work stations in the office? What is ultimately done with the paper?

Then you go back and ask the obvious questions about the answers you found to each of the foregoing ones. Why does the paper exist in the first place? Is it actually needed? Are all those copies needed? Why? Do all those people need to handle it? If so, could their work stations be arranged in closer proximity? Does any person handle the paper more than once? If so, could both handlings be done in one operation? What could have been eliminated? Combined? Rearranged? Changed in sequence? It sounds like the work simplification steps, doesn't it? And that's right.

Some astute, profit-minded individual once observed. "Think of each piece of paper as it comes in as being coated with a *thin veneer of gold*. Each time it is handled, a bit of the veneer is rubbed off and lost. That veneer represents profit. The more handlings, the less profit."

Now, as I recall, he was actually speaking of orders coming into a company, but the analogy holds in a large measure for all pieces of paper handled. For handling papers requires people and time — and people and time cost money. It could be that you are losing your thin veneer of profit through too many handlings of certain pieces of paper. Get everybody on the staff interested in reducing the handling of *each piece of paper*. Get any good office management book and study the chapters on work organization. They invariably tackle the flow of paper as one means of improving work organization. If yours is a large office, it might pay to call in an office consultant. And just as you can get into the habit of thinking PERT, you can also become conscious of that *thin*

82

veneer of gold getting rubbed off and lost every time you handle a paper needlessly.

Forms

Analyze the forms used. Are the items to be typed on the forms arranged in time-saving fashion? No need to use the line-space adjuster, for example. Are items to be filled in blocked insofar as possible to save tab-stopping frequently or back-spacing? Do multiple copies provide for one-time entry of data items? Ask the employees who work on the forms to give their suggestions for time-saving ideas, both on the arrangement of the forms and their handling. Again read what the office management books have to say.

Space

Consider rearranging the office space. If your analysis of flow of work shows much "traveling" distance for any papers, try to cut down distances by a different arrangement. Again, those office management books come in handy. The hard way is to just start with the furniture. An easier way is to draw up some cardboard or paper templates, scaled to size of whatever scale you use for your scale diagram of the floor space, and push around these paper bits instead. You can try all sorts of new arrangements right on a desk top. Let everybody get into the act. This may even be the time to scrap some inefficient furniture for some newer, modular desks. Incidentally, you'll be surprised at the good ideas those women employees can come up with on rearranging the office. What woman doesn't love moving the furniture for a new look — even when the criterion is improved efficiency?

Know Your Operation

Come to grips with the problem of analyzing office jobs. In any office situation whoever manages the operation should know what systems and procedures are carried out, what jobs and personnel are required, what qualifications are necessary, how much should be paid for the work done in each of the jobs — and certainly the comparable relationship between those jobs. Somebody has to set up priorities of what is worth more than something else. What is it that you are paying the highest price for? (Remember that admonition about not utilizing high-priced help for low-priced work?) Sometimes, when you start analyzing those jobs, you are in for some big surprises, especially in small offices where job analysis has been given short shrift. If "everybody does everything" in your office, then maybe everybody ought to get about the same pay with a little extra thrown in here and there. Certain people get a little extra, say, Mrs. Oldone, who has been here the longest (seniority), Mrs. Ayebee, who has a college degree (education), and Miss Whistlebait, who is easily the most photogenic (no explanation needed). Just how do you equate requirements of the job and job performance with the going rate on that job, anyway? And what are you willing to pay the highest rate for?

"My pay scale is strictly along lines of business brought in — *sales* made," said one agency manager. "My business is on computer. I can tell you at the end of every day exactly what each girl has sold that day and for all the days up to then. I give raises periodically, whenever she reaches a certain quota. The girls know they get raises in line with sales accomplished. No, they don't know the quotas I establish, but they know when they've met one because that's when they get a raise. Funny thing. Immediately after she gets a raise, a girl invariably drops a bit in the sales volume she brings in. Then after that initial slump, her sales begin to climb again. I've learned to expect a decrease in a girl's sales immediately after she gets a raise, though it always seemed to me that the raise ought to be an incentive for her to work harder right away."

In that agency the criterion for pay was well spelled out. Perhaps you use the same yardstick. If you do, just be sure that each employee has equal time at the points of contact where possibilities for sales come in. Does each girl have the same opportunity at the phone lines if phone lines bring in more business than the counter? Or vice versa? If sales are your criterion for pay incentives, are the opportunities for achieving sales equal within the office situation? What happens to someone like that girl who was told, "Don't sell any place you haven't been"? We are not decrying "sales" as a criterion for equating what you pay for, but rather making a plea that you analyze the sales opportunities for each person if that is how you measure whether or not an individual is worth a raise.

84

"But even when I know what each girl does, it is hard to put a price on it," someone says. "You just can't measure what's done the way you can in an industrial plant, for example, where the work is highly repetitive and where many workers do exactly the same thing. It just isn't that standardized in a small office."

Right you are. And you've come up with two good reasons why work measurement in an office is difficult. (1) The nature of the work entails much nonrepetitive work, and (2) the element of mental effort is more variable and difficult to measure. But in spite of the difficulties, attempts can be made to classify and rate the various aspects of office jobs.

Rating Tools

1. *Job analysis* — gathering information concerning the job and trying to break it down into its various elements.

2. *Job description* — taking the data from the job analysis and presenting it in an organized form that tells what the job is like in terms of its requirements.

3. *Job specification* — recording the qualifications that the worker must have to do the job. Actually, job descriptions and job specification could be combined, but they are frequently separated for the reason that job description describes the job while job specification describes the worker needed to do the job.

4. *Job evaluation* — classifying, ranking, and grading jobs in order to set a pay scale on each in relation to other jobs.

5. *Work measurement and setting job standards* — determining the requirements and the criteria by which performance of tasks may be measured.

You take a look at those five techniques and probably mutter, "So what have they got to do with an office the size of mine?" Then add after a moment, perhaps, "Hmmmm. If each of us did some of that time analysis we were talking about for his particular job, we would be well started on that No. 1. And if we made those pie charts of how each person spends his time, we'd have some good data for No. 2. And from that — well, it wouldn't be difficult to do No. 3. I guess we could have a go at it."

Good. And when you start translating those pie charts that resulted

85

from your time checks into job descriptions and job specifications, ask questions such as these, and write down the answers in orderly fashion.

About the job:

What are the routine tasks performed? Daily? Weekly? Monthly?

What are the special tasks?

What percentage of time would you judge goes into each of the various tasks? ("Got it right on this pie chart, boss!")

About the worker:

What experience?

How much orientation and training should be given?

Where does the job lead?

That won't be difficult to do, will it? And you will have clipped off the first three of those techniques with the help of your staff for each of the jobs in the office. You've already decided to ignore No. 5, so that leaves No. 4, *Job Evaluation*, staring you in the face.

Job evaluation is tougher to do. But with some job descriptions and job specifications, you can begin to come to a decision about what each job is worth with something more to go on than that Mrs. Wrinkles has seniority, etc. The larger your organization, the more important it is that employees doing similar work are paid approximately the same salary.

You can debate that last statement if you want to, for there are all sorts of factors inherent in the individual that influence an employee's worth to an organization, and there is another group, such as cost of living, competitive salaries in your particular marketplace, etc. But if you are serious about wanting to evaluate jobs as a partial basis for knowing what work performance you are paying for and whether you are paying adequately or extravagantly for services performed, you need to have a go at some kind of job evaluation.

Methods of evaluating jobs can be divided into two classifications:

Nonquantitative – ranking method and job classification method
Quantitative – factor comparison method and point method

Office analysts suggest that in offices with up to 30 or 40 employees the nonquantitative methods may be effectively used. After that, you probably need to go to more quantitative methods since not enough raters will be familiar with all the jobs.

"Good," you say. "The nonquantitative ones look a lot easier to do. Let's have a capsule review of them."

The *ranking* method is just what it implies — ranking jobs in order of their relative importance according to difficulty and responsibility, and hence in importance to the organization. It usually follows that jobs are ranked in importance to job titles. The agency manager gets the top pay, the assistant manager, next, etc. The old RHIP (rank has its privileges) was never truer than in this privilege to receive more pay than the next ranking individual. In a small office a mere ranking classification may work quite well, provided the components of job hierarchy are kept in line with the title. Certainly it is easily understood, albeit it is so subjective that sometimes the titles of the jobs, rather than what is done by the ones holding those titles, become the determining factor in the pay scale. If that happens in your office, you may be headed for dissatisfaction with your salary scale. So if you use the ranking system, be certain that you pay for *performance* as well as title when you set up the monetary evaluation of the various jobs.

It probably should be mentioned in passing, that although the ranking system may work well for you and is certainly the easiest to use, it is being used less and less in businesses today. Possibly the most popular method today, especially in large businesses, is the point method, which is one of those quantitative methods that we aren't going into here.

The *job classification method* grows out of the ranking system and is the sort of thing the civil service has arrived at in its multiplicity of *grades*, each of which has a base and an ending scale. It has the advantage of definiteness. Employees know where they stand once they are on a certain grade level, and they can usually see that the nature of the work has been combined with the salary range and that there is a direct relationship between the rating of the importance of the job and the salary paid. It has the disadvantage of a certain inflexibility that must be stretched quite out of shape at times if cost of living, supply and demand of competitive firms, etc. are to be handled reasonably and to the best interest of the agency. If the inflexibility is completely lost or becomes a sham that is all too readily discerned by the employees, the employees will soon lose confidence in the company's policies.

There is no magic formula or technique that will work for all offices. But if you are going to organize the work in your organization on any kind of monetary basis that is equitable, you would do well to find out what you are paying for in terms of work performed.

Analyze Office Costs

Analyze your office costs in the light of your gross business. Your net profit. How in or out of line are they? What are the extenuating circumstances that account for certain out-of-line items? There may be some. For example, if your office space cost is extremely high for the reason that you must remain in a high-rent location because that is where you must be to do a good business, then it is justifiable. One way of analyzing office costs is to break them down on a basis of "per square feet of office space" cost. Take each cost, item by item, and subject it to the severest scrutiny. Consult your local Administrative Management Society for statistics they have compiled for office costs in your area. How do you stack up? Can you afford to cut down on certain items? Or increase them? Often so simple an improvement as increased or improved lighting in the office will result in a correlating increase in profits far in excess of the cost of the lighting.

And having analyzed the "environmental" costs, you are back to the problem of effecting savings through more efficient work procedures.

Analyze Gross Business

Analyze your gross business in light of your profits. What portions of your gross business bring you high returns in profits? What portions "actually cost you money?"

"I'd really like to scrap my domestic business," one agency manager said. "I'd be farther ahead. Why, I could cut this operation back to a one-man operation, run it from my home, take just a certain number of big tours a year, and have time for my family and myself as well. It would be exciting and fun. But I can't do that to my clients. They deserve the domestic service they utilize and need. Besides, if I abandon the domestic part, those clients that come to me for international travel

88

would probably take *all* their business to the fellow who handled their domestic travel. So I'm caught with handling both myself."

Perhaps his problem, and yours as well, is to increase the *ratio* of international to domestic business. Freeing your best employees of routine small tasks and aiding them to work aggressively on international business may be one of the reorganization facets you should look into. You could be paying too much for the handling of the low per cent business. Keep asking yourself, "What are my highest-paid employees doing? My lowest paid?" The answers to those questions may give you a good basis for work reorganization.

The Built-in Helpers

Be alert to the little shortcuts and time-savers. Certainly we should say again that "It's the little things that make the big difference" applies to any work organization and improvement program. Many of your employees have developed excellent small shortcuts of one kind or another. Give them credit for being on the smart side when they come up with one of these and watch them think up others.

We saw one staff that had come up with a simple little trick that saved much time and, undoubtedly, frustration when it came to recording the tax and subtotal figures on just *two* copies of tickets instead of all copies, as you were allowed to do before July 1, 1970. They simply completed all four copies of the ticket in the usual manner with the exception of those two figures. Just before recording those two figures, they slip the 3 x 5 work card, on which they have figured the fare, *behind* the first two pages of the ticket so that it blocks out the last two pages upon which those figures can no longer be shown. (Surely somebody will get around to seeing to it that that corner is *non*carbonized on all but the first copy when the forms catch up with the regulations.) Then being sure that the side of the card on which they have done the fare figuring is facing the carbonized back of copy two, they write or type in those missing figures which now will appear on only the first two copies and the 3 x 5 card. Which are exactly the places where they want them to appear. *One* recording does the job, including the blocking out, and getting the tax and subtotal on the working card, too. Neat. And it also saves errors in copying, as the girl pointed out.

89

"You have to block out those last two copies with something," she said. "But if you do it with anything except the card on which you have done the figuring, you have to take time to record it there, too. Of course you want to be sure you get it on the back side of the card instead of the front," she said with a grin.

Incidentally, those 3 x 5 cards, printed or duplicated on the front sides with spaces for recording flights, arrivals, departures, dates, etc. are a neat bit of work organization in themselves. Especially when the reverse side is used for figuring the fares for the flights recorded on the front side. Everything is all ready for recording on the ticket and for verifying by the accountant in one easy spot.

The same girl who showed me the card trick had some work routines that must have contributed greatly to the smooth operation of both the small branch office in which she was employed and in the main office. In answer to my question, "How far is your work divided along functional lines, or is there no opportunity for that in a one-girl situation such as this?" she replied, "Some of it is according to function." And added, "And it works out rather well. For example, on my way to work each morning I pick up all the agency mail at the post office. I bring it here, not to the main office. I sort and analyze. Anything that I can handle — some mornings I can take care of it all — I answer. Those letters and carbons are filed here, too, for if there is additional correspondence or a phone call concerning it, I'll need the information here. Anything that I think Mr. Smith has to handle, I put in a folder like this, right on the corner of the desk. He spends a part of each day out here. Just as he leaves, that folder goes *swoosh* into his briefcase. Later on, down at the main agency, there is a work-study girl (co-op) who comes in to handle any dictation he has. She takes care of the filing down there, too."

"How do you *index* that correspondence you take care of here?" I asked.

"By name of person writing," she replied quickly. For that's the way I'll look for it or refer to it."

"Good girl," I thought. "She knows the one about 'Not where do you file it but *where would you look for it*?', should be your first question when you index materials for filing."

"How often do you clean out those files?" I asked.

"It depends — " she said. (There we go again — *climate* and *terrain*.) "But usually, if there has been nothing for the past three months on something, I pitch." Good organization again. Getting rid of useless papers in the file is excellent. "Do you do that on your own initiative?" I asked. "Certainly," she said. "That's one of the things I like about this job. I'm up to my ears in work — all the time. There's so much to do — to keep up with — if I hadn't worked for the airlines before I came here, I sometimes wonder how I'd do it. But I like having to figure things out and make decisions. But for someone who hadn't the kind of experience I had, it might be more difficult. But those seminars the airlines hold are marvelous."

The Carrier Helpers

I'd heard that one before. In fact, every girl I talked with mentioned how helpful those seminars and ticket schools were. Even the one who competently ran a branch office so far removed from the main office that she really did handle everything, including the banking and financial records for the branch, thought the seminars and ticket schools were training programs she couldn't have done without. "I don't know how in the world a new girl coming into an agency office would ever learn it all," she said. "It's hard enough to keep up with it when you've had years of experience. But those seminars and ticket schools are wonderful. I just wish there were more of them and that we could attend oftener."

Certainly I heard that sentiment expressed often enough that it ought to be spelled out as a guideline for effecting better work organization for travel agencies. So here it is:

Make every possible use you can of the helps the airlines give you in training employees. Enough said! No, not quite. Why not tell them the story of the girl who couldn't "sell any place she hadn't been" — complete with a few sobbing violins in the background? And perhaps more expense-paid trips for beginning employees will become as much the order of things as are ticket seminars and schools. I'd not dismiss it with a scoffing, "Dreamer!" I'd work on it if I were you. It would probably be money in their pockets as well as yours in the long run.

The Association Helpers

Utilize every possible help you can get from ASTA, ICTA, and any other associations to which you belong. If you aren't making use of every bit of information that comes out of your associations that is applicable to your particular situation, you just must be trying *not* to succeed in business. The application blank and the correspondence course mentioned earlier are two examples of the excellent help available from ASTA, for example.

Take a bit of initiative and ask for help in areas in which you feel you could use some. A well-directed letter or two suggesting areas in which you need some professional help might be just the spur needed to get such action initiated and completed. For example, *filing* in various agencies was spotted as an area in which some reorganization would come in mighty handy.

You'll be interested to know, I think, that almost invariably, whenever a girl was asked if there were any special headaches or frustrations in connection with her work, something or other about those files came into the conversation. So if you haven't already done so, why not write to your associations suggesting that help in *filing* would certainly be welcomed?

There —

That's all we're going to say about work organization. If you're feeling somewhat like the little boy who replied to his father (upon being told to go ask his mother the answer to some question), "But, Daddy, I really don't want to know that much about it," remember that you don't have to put it *all* into practice. Not unless you want to. None of it, for that matter. But if you'd pick out at least one or two suggestions that are particularly adaptable to your agency's *climate* and *terrain*, you might find yourself with happier, less fatigued employees, more satisfied and returning customers, and a larger margin of profit. It could happen. But you won't know until you try.

Chapter 5

Profit Planning through Correct Accounting Practices

by

Richard F. Cook

The Professional Manager and Accounting

A responsible agency manager and executive is obliged to find methods which will result in a strong financial picture for his agency. Accounting and bookkeeping are not normally among the exotic reasons that draw one into the travel agency industry. However, if you desire that black bottom line at the end of the year, they are a very necessary function of management.

To encourage further reading, let's eliminate most of the double-entry, credit, debit language which may tend to discourage those who find accounting tedious. Instead, we will deal specifically with the *results* we wish to obtain from our bookkeeping systems, as well as some of the *methods* used to produce these results. We will look at the way these results can be used to budget for profit, search for a meaningful definition of that confusing term "cash flow," find methods of controlling receivables, and study the effects of new personnel as related to our profit picture.

Bookkeeping Systems

This chapter will not address itself extensively to the methods of keeping books. There are, in reality, almost as many systems as there are types of agents. These systems vary from the very elementary single entry to the most sophisticated computerized systems, with literally dozens of systems in between.

There is however, one basic system which seems to be the most applicable to the majority of agents, particularly those whose volume does not warrant a computerized system. While there are many variations of this system, it is known in the accounting industry as "pegboard" bookkeeping. Pegboard bookkeeping derives its name from the use of a metal board with small pegs on its left margin. The system almost always is based on using a client record card, upon which is entered every payment received from the client and every payment made in his behalf. This client record card is carefully aligned on the board, with carbon placed in between (unneccessary when sensitized paper is used). When the entry is made on the client record card, a copy of it is made on the sales (receipts) journal page (which is placed between the carbon and the board) or in the disbursement journal. Some systems allow checks to be written, thereby having client record and disbursement journal entries as a by-product.

This system is commendable in that it does an excellent job of obtaining account receivable records. It also seems wise to make one entry rather than two or three. Not only is time (and consequently, money) saved, but errors are cut to a minimum. Other excellent systems for modest-sized agencies are also available, however. Consult your C.P.A. for advice.

Bookkeeping and Accounting Functions

Bookkeeping should be an internal function of all travel agencies. On the other hand, unless you are large enough to be blessed with a qualified accountant on your staff, the actual accounting function should be done professionally on the outside. This distinction between bookkeeping and accounting can be defined even further: assuming that all bookkeeping entries are processed internally and your books have been developed to incorporate operating information useful to management, then the results of this information should also be gathered internally, meaning that you, the owner or manager, can produce your own monthly profit and loss statement.

Your outside accountant should be charged with the necessary responsibility of producing your balance sheet and doing your tax work. However, the more accounting data you can produce accurately with your internal staff, the less you will spend on accounting overhead. Needless to say, if these records are not being produced internally by you or your staff accurately and on time (a monthly profit and loss statement is essential), because of lack of time, then the outside accountant and his related cost of producing these necessary records must be a part of your budget.

A periodic audit by the firm's C.P.A. is highly recommended. This is important for security reasons and also to warn the manager of inherent dangers — a warning which could avoid a costly failure.

Accounts Receivable

The system you use should produce at least monthly (preferably more often) an accounts receivable aging report. This should show who owes you money, how much and how tardy they are in settling their obligations.

This record should be a by-product of your bookkeeping. It cannot be kept accurately through notations on client files or through an open-receivable file. (This is a central file where all unpaid invoices are placed, removing those invoices when they are paid, and leaving what remains in file as "open receivables.") There are two distinct shortcomings to the open receivable system — filing errors and dishonesty. Both should be convincing enough to require, in addition, a client receipt and payment record which must be part of your basic system. Unless you use this system to produce accounts receivable aging reports, you might as well not keep the records.

While we are discussing the receivable problem, we might as well consider ways to avoid receivables. Cash and credit cards are obviously the answer. The trend toward the use of bank credit cards as well as those designed for travel and entertainment, while occasionally placing an additional work load on your staff, is very encouraging. In accepting credit cards, most or all of your receivable problem is eliminated.

If you feel that credit privileges must be granted, see that your staff has well-defined policies as to who may receive credit. Now that credit has been granted in a standardized manner, you must be willing to get tough in order to collect the monies owed. On 5, 6, 7, and even 11 per cent commissions few bad debts can be afforded. Furthermore, a client cannot be allowed to refuse to pay because his trip did not live up to his expectations, for reasons frequently beyond your control. For that reason, it is poor policy to permit credit on hotel and tour sales. Large agencies that are forced to extend credit on a wide scale basis would be wise to investigate the Dun and Bradstreet Collection Service.

Those agents whose receivables are less than their monthly commissions should be commended. You can not get hurt too badly if you loan only your own money!

One other way to control your credit is to charge clients 1-2 per cent per month for outstanding balances over 15 to 30 days duration.

This is standard procedure for many agents. However, before adopting this policy, check your state laws to see if it is permissable, and the manner in which it is permitted.

Bank Checks

Many of the agency's most important records will be by-products of your check-writing system. Even if this is not an accounting form, half of your accounting originates from the check book. Many agents do not take advantage of checks that can be custom printed and designed to save time for them and their staff. One or more of the following designs can be easily incorporated into your system resulting in substantial economies.

1. *Voucher checks:* The voucher check is normally slightly larger than twice the size of a normal check. It is divided horizontally with a perforation, with the actual check on one half and a large enough space on the other to allow for a message to be typed as well as show calculations for the transaction. Since this message portion is detached by the supplier when he receives payment, it eliminates the need to type an accompanying letter. And the calculations showing deposit, gross, commission and net figures make an easy job of entries for the bookkeeper. Since these checks are available in triplicate form, the original and actual check goes to the supplier, the second copy becomes the "stub" and is kept in a check binder, in numerical sequence, and the third becomes another record in your client's file.

2. *Window check:* These checks are designed so that the name of the party and his address can be typed in a space that fits a window envelope, again eliminating the extra step of typing an envelope. Voucher checks are frequently designed to incorporate this feature.

3. *Sensitized checks:* For those agents who use the pegboard bookkeeping system, it is possible to order checks with a carbon-sensitized portion, allowing the actual writing of the check to become an entry in the bookkeeping system at the same time.

From your disbursements (bank checks) a determination can be made of business generated for hotels, airlines, steamships, tour companies, etc., the commissions earned, and where your operating expenses have been directed. In addition, air reports will determine volume by commission categories. Most of the information required for Profit and Loss Statements will come from your disbursement records.

Improving Management through Figures

Let's take a close look at some of the information worth developing as by-products of an effective bookkeeping system. The following categories can produce valuable reference material necessary for good management.

1. *Gross volume earned per employee:* Every employer should be aware of the individual production of each employee. There are arguments to the contrary, including those who say, "I don't want my employees to compete for the good clients," "I want teamwork in my office," "I have no incentive commission plan, so why should I bother?" "I want all my clients to receive equal service," "Let's not ruin the *esprit de corps,*" and many others. However, no matter how good a friend or salesman that employee is, he must be responsive to profit. A few pleasant, but unprofitable, employees may lead you down the road to insolvency. Furthermore, employees must produce in proportion to total salaries versus total overhead, or you will soon find yourself earning all the necessary income to support unprofitable staff members. When this point is reached, there will be no time "to manage" and your growth will decline as rapidly as your profits.

2. *Gross earnings (commissions) by type of sale:* There is a multitude of different, possible breakdowns. Listed is my preferred breakdown:

Domestic Air Commissions
    5%
    6%
    7%
    8%
   10%
   11%

Domestic Tours (without air) Commissions
International Air Commissions
    7%
   10%

Foreign Tour Sales Commissions (without air)
Steamship and Cruise Sales Commissions
Direct Hotel Commissions
Miscellaneous Commissions (car rentals, insurance, etc.)
Service Charges
Group Tours Commissions

When your agency promotes any group tours, these should be further broken down by commission for each tour, even though you may not actually operate the tour. Also, records should be kept of total tour sales of each tour operator. We also recommend accounts be kept of any special event that is not an annual happening, such as World Fairs, the Olympics, religious celebrations, sporting events, and so on. Again this breakdown applies to the groups, not individuals.

Gross Sales for Large Suppliers

This category is not considered essential. However, many agents wish to keep an account of their volume by carrier or tour company. While this may give the agent some satisfaction and may further aid in securing peak season space, it is at best, in the case of the airlines, inaccurate. Airline revenue accounting is necessary to produce exact figures, so I question the time spent versus the results. Since the airlines do keep their own production records, it appears that these would be sufficient. For other suppliers and principals, it would be less time consuming to go through the duplicate set of bank check vouchers with an adding machine tape to arrive at the totals. This is the method many agencies use in securing their gross sales with those tour companies giving an over-ride commission. It is important to be aware of the commission plateaus as you approach them.

There are other breakdowns that might be helpful, such as sales by geographical areas of destination, sales of advertised products, new sales versus repeat customer sales, and similar categories. Before producing such data to find these answers, you must weigh the time expended against the profitable use of the results.

Disbursement Information

Depending upon the individual system presently used, much sales information has been derived from the disbursement journal. In addition to this information, a careful accounting of your operating expenses is required. It is extremely important that the entire travel agency industry arrive at some standardization in categories of operating expenses. Hundreds of industries, including the closely allied hotel and motel industry, have been printing comparisons of operating expenses by size of operation, geographic location, etc., for many years. Without these standardized categories our industry will be unable to develop meaningful data.

The following is a list of expense categories and explanations as to what they should include. A more detailed breakdown can be made by adding sub-categories.

1. *Salary Overhead:* To be fully aware of personnel overhead this category should include:
   a. Actual salaries paid (may be divided into management, sales, sales and comissions and non-sales)
   b. Employer's contributions to social security, unemployment insurance, workman's compensation, pension plans, health and other insurance plans that are directly proportionate to the number of employees and/or total payroll.
2. *Occupancy Cost:* This category, which is very useful when considering new or expanded quarters, should include:
   a. Rent, or depreciation if self-owned
   b. Utilities (light, heat, etc.)
   c. Leasehold improvements
   d. Office cleaning
   e. Repairs and maintenance.
3. *Advertising and Promotions:* This all-inclusive category covers all the things you do to bring customers to your agency. It should include entertainment expenses, brochures, and even dues to clubs you belong to for exposure purposes.
   a. Media advertising (radio, newspaper, TV, etc.)
   b. Direct mail cost (printing, supplies and postage attributable to direct mail)
   c. Trade shows
   d. Window displays
   e. Telephone directory advertising

f. Travel and entertainment related to promotion
g. Brochures and printing
h. Dues to clubs used for promotional purposes
i. Giveaways
j. Less rebates on advertising due to co-op arrangements.

4. *Telephone and Telegraph:* Please note that the total is a net figure after deducting amount for reimbursed telephone and cable expenses.
a. Telephone (local calls and equipment)
b. Telephone (long distance)
c. Telegraph, teletype and cables
d. Direct line costs to major accounts or airlines
e. Less reimbursed telephone and cable tolls paid by clients.

5. *Office Supplies and Equipment:*
a. Stationery
b. Forms and other printed matter used for operation
c. Subscriptions to guides and manuals
d. Equipment depreciation
Equipment rental.

6. *Postage, Freight and Delivery:*
a. Postage other than direct mail use
b. Freight
c. Ticket delivery costs.

7. *Education:* This category is important, for as your business becomes more complex, education will play an increasing part. If we budget for education costs, we will become more cognizant of their relative importance.
a. Orientation travel
b. Schools and seminars
c. On-the-job training (overtime, food, etc.).

8. *Miscellaneous:* May be broken down into several categories.
a. Taxes other than employee, corporate and income taxes
b. Professional services (accounting, legal, etc.)
c. General insurance
d. ATC Bond
e. Bad debt, error and collection costs
f. Trade association dues and costs.

Finding Weak Spots through Comparisons

Because agents throughout the country have often expressed a desire to compare their profit picture with other agents, a Profit and Loss Statement is presented here that can easily be used for such a purpose. These figures do not come from one particular agency. They are the result of a personal study of approximately 50 travel agencies, in addition to studying a similar set of percentages of expenses as produced by the Touche, Ross, Bailey, and Smart Cost Study. Since the Cost Study statistics were averages of successful and unsuccessful agents, I have adjusted the figures so that the resulting Profit and Loss Statement can belong to a *moderately* successful agency. No one wants to compare his P & L Statement with that of an agency operating in the red!

While the total volume of an agency is relatively unimportant, for the sake of clarity, let us assume that the gross earnings (commissions) of our XYZ Agency total $50,000. The approximate percentages of the expenses are also shown so adjustments to these figures for comparison purposes can be made.

Many agents judge their business by gross sales rather than commissions. If this applies to you and you will be estimating these percentages, consider that 8 per cent to 8 1/2 per cent commission on gross sales would be a good average. This reflects the 1969 domestic air commission structure. This estimate is high for those specializing in commercial accounts and low for those concentrating on group tours, so adjust accordingly to fit your type of agency business. In the following P & L Statement the commission figure for domestic air is including 5, 6, 7, 8, 10 and 11 per cent commission rates, although the breakdown of each separate category has been omitted.

The figures at right show a respectable *net* income for the agent of average size. It is well to note that all costs have been figured as a percentage of gross income (commission). This has been done so that the agent earning $100,000 in commission can easily double these figures for comparison purposes. The agent earning $25,000 can cut the figures in half. Using the percentages shown, any agent can compare P & L's. It should further be noted that the larger the agent becomes, the more efficient he should be, and therefore it is recommended that any

PROFIT & LOSS STATEMENT- XYZ AGENCY
Fiscal Year January 1 to December 31

GROSS INCOME (COMMISSIONS)

Domestic air	$12,500.00	
International air	13,500.00	
Domestic tours	1,000.00	
International tours	7,200.00	
Steamship and Cruises	4,700.00	
Hotels	1,900.00	
Miscellaneous	1,100.00	
Service charges	600.00	
Group tours (air and ground)	7,500.00	
Gross Income		$50,000.00

EXPENSES

Employment Costs			
Management	$10,000.00		
Staff	15,700.00		
Fringe Benefits	1,800.00		
Total employment costs (55%)		27,500.00	
Occupancy (7%)		3,500.00	
Advertising & promotion (8%)		4,000.00	
Office supplies & equipment (5%)		2,500.00	
Telephone & telegraph (5%)		2,500.00	
Education & orient. travel (3%)		1,500.00	
Postage, freight, delivery (2%)		1,000.00	
Miscellaneous (5)		2,500.00	
Total Expenses			$45,000.00
Net Profit			$5,000.00

agent doing $100,000 in commissions should attempt to reduce his cost of personnel by 2 to 3 per cent and add this amount to profit. Somewhere around $150,000 in commission, the travel agent should lower personnel cost to 50 per cent and show a net profit.

These figures are not intended to be absolute minimum costs. There are agents who operate with personnel costs as low as 35 per cent. The intention here is to avoid the exceptions and not talk the ultimate, but, instead, talk about what is being attained in many good agencies across the country.

Note that the net profit happened to work out to 10 per cent of the Gross Earnings in this P & L. Your operation can be measured against these figures, although there will be some instances where your figures may vary for special reasons, such as the following:

1. Frequently Occupancy and Advertising may be lumped together using 15 per cent as a total for the two categories. Some agents pay a premium price for ground floor space and consider, rightfully, a portion of this rent as advertising. Other agents may choose lower rental areas in order to allow for higher promotion costs.

2. Some agents have effectively developed word-of-mouth advertising at no cost, and I hope that this difference shows on their "bottom line".

3. As automation becomes a part of your operation, personnel costs and telephone expenses drop percentagewise, while equipment costs increase.

Employment Costs

The cost of employment in the average travel agency actually is closer to 60 per cent than the 55 per cent I have used in the example of a *successful* agency.

If the XYZ Agency in our example P & L Statement were to feel the dire need of another employee at this point in his growth, and that employee were to cost him $7,000 per year, his operation would immediately go from a profit of $5,000 to a loss of $2,000, unless the agent were able to generate sufficient additional business to support that employee and the additional overhead incurred by that employee. Using an employment cost of 55 per cent of total earnings, it would appear that an additional $7,000 employee would have to earn $12,700 in commissions or an increased gross earnings of 25.4 percent to still show a $5,000 profit.

It is difficult for an agency to grow at this rate without very careful planning, and that means budgeting. It may be that the agency's normal annual growth is 15 per cent, so he is then going to have to find ways to spend his promotion budget or increase it in order to show this unusual increase.

Budgeting

A properly planned budget is not only one of the travel agent's most important financial tools but it is also a valuable marketing technique. Budgeting is simply the act of making a management decision based on the increase in gross commissions expected; considering any increased commissions as determined by principals, past growth, new or expanded office quarters, addition of new staff, or increased advertising costs, and any other factors that will affect gross sales and gross commissions. The second step is to adjust your expenses accordingly, relating them to the above factors or inflation. Some agents may be able to make these estimates based on prior years experience and never have to go into the detail shown here. On the other hand, by the example mentioned previously, it can be seen that the addition of one person at the improper time can drastically change your profit picture. A mistake of this type can be avoided by modern budgeting practices.

In order to derive the greatest benefits from your budgeting efforts, it is essential that both your monthly and end-of-the-year P & L Statements contain as much detail as possible. Your books may not show these breakdowns, but the method remains the same, even if you are forced to go back and delve into your books to come up with these answers.

Again, using our XYZ Agency Profit and Loss Statement, shown previously, we will work with the gross income figure of $50,000 for our example. This total will be high for some agents and low for others, but serves as a figures that will be easy to convert in comparing your own individual figures. A given fiscal year of January 1 to December 31 will be used.

We could work directly from the figures on our example and make fair estimates of increases in overhead for the coming year, and increases in sales and commissions for the same period. The disadvantage, however, is that you do not know how well you are doing until the end of the coming fiscal year. Therefore it is recommended that your entire budgeting procedure be a month-to-month effort with a quarterly (end of each three months) review, at which time you can commit yourself to take any necessary action on any new or unexpected trend that very often appears in this changing world.

The following chart shows our P & L Statement for three months and the total for the quarter. The entire exercise described below should be applied to each month of the fiscal year prior to the beginning of that year.

Each month, as you receive the prior month's P & L Statement, you should review it against your projected budget. Give your budget information to your accountant so he can show budget and results alongside of each other on your P & L. At the same time, he should prepare year-to-date figures for both results and budget. If your result versus budget is too far apart, adjustments must be made accordingly. Consider the quarterly statements as an absolute deadline to take action on declining sales or profits, unproductive personnel, skyrocketing telephone or supply costs, or others.

The sample P & L Statement is shown for the first quarter of the fiscal year. The budget is in two parts: 1) A marketing or commission budget, and 2) An expense budget. Marketing or sales decisions are made first. In arriving at the annual budget for earnings, use the following considerations. These guidelines should be of assistance in planning for each year. The real purpose of including this exercise is that marketing and sales planning are vital to our financial planning.

Domestic Air: The agent in question has had receivable problems from a few of his commercial accounts. He has decided to resign 20 per cent of his commercial accounts. His normal growth in the past has been 10 per cent so he has budgeted income approximately 10 per cent less than the prior year.

International Air: As part of his market planning, the agent has decided to do a direct mail piece to companies with international divisions and to follow up on this mailing with personal calls. His anticipated increase is 20 per cent.

Domestic Tour Sales: Due to his decision to eliminate his unprofitable domestic air accounts, he will probably break about even on tour sales between those he may lose due to de-emphasis of domestic sales and his normal 10 per cent gain in business.

International Tour Sales: Through his direct mail campaign and increased emphasis on international air he has decided to aim for a 20 per cent international tour growth.

Steamship & Cruises: Has shown same growth as in previous years.

Hotel Commissions: This agent has decided that the reduced cost of reserving hotels (through WATS lines) will make it worth his while to attempt to book hotels for all his commercial clients and any inquiries off the street. He then budgeted a 30 per cent increase.

Service Charges: Our agent has decided to institute a service and cancellation policy that will reasonably off-set some of his costs in this area (refer to this subject as discussed at the end of this chapter).

Group Tours: For many agents this category of profit can make or break a year. The first big step has been taken when this profit category is separated from other commission listings. The agent must go through several mental exercises to properly budget his group tours:

1. Can I repeat the tour at the same time with a reasonable chance of success?

2. If it was a once-in-a-lifetime movement, can something else be developed to replace the income?

3. What effect will increased advertising of specific tours have on my net profit?

4. Is there a special event next year that will give me the opportunity of increasing the number of tours operated?

5. Can I spread out my tour activities to attract income in normally unprofitable months?

6. Am I charging prices that return the proper profit?

Our agent has considered these factors and arrived at a budget increase in September and November, as well as a decrease for October. He has spread out his work load in a more even fashion.

XYZ AGENCY
Profit and Loss Statement
First Quarter

	January	February	March	Total First Quarter
Domestic Air Commission	1000-	1300-	1200-	3500-
International Air Comm.	1000-	900-	700-	2600-
Domestic Tour Comm.	80-	140-	60-	280-
International Tour Comm.	550-	550-	400-	1500-
Steamship and Cruises	580-	710-	590-	1880-
Hotel Commissions	190-	180-	130-	500-
Miscellaneous	70-	90-	40-	200-
Service Charges	45-	55-	50-	150-
Group Tours (Air and Ground)	1500-	2800-		4300-
TOTAL GROSS INCOME	5015-	6725-	3170-	14910-
Employment Costs	2300-	2300-	2300-	6900-
Occupancy	290-	290-	300-	880-
Advertising and Promotion	800-	800-	400-	2000-
Office Supplies and Equipment	200-	200-	200-	600-
Telephone and Telegraph	200-	200-	200-	600-
Education	300-	300-	300-	900-
Postage, Freight, & Delivery	70-	80-	70-	220-
Miscellaneous	200-	200-	200-	600-
TOTAL EXPENSES	4360-	4370-	3970-	12700-
NET INCOME	655-	2355-	(800-)	2210-

Profit and Loss Budget
First Quarter

January	February	March	Total First Quarter
900-	1170-	1080-	3150-
1200-	1080-	840-	3120-
80-	140-	60-	280-
660-	660-	480-	1800
640	780-	650-	2070-
250-	240-	170-	660-
90-	120-	50-	260-
90-	110-	100-	300-
2400-	2100-	1500-	6000-
6310-	6400-	4930-	17640-
2530-	2530-	2530-	7590-
300-	300-	300-	900-
1000-	1000-	400-	2400-
240-	240-	240-	720-
190-	190-	190-	570-
300-	300-	300-	900-
90-	100-	90-	280-
240-	240	240-	720-
4890-	4900-	4290-	14080-
1420-	1500-	640-	3560-

Scanning the total sales projection, our XYZ Agency has budgeted an 18.3 per cent increase in gross earnings or commissions.

Let us now examine his projected expenses and his reasons for arriving at these figures

Employment Costs: This agent has increased his commissions for these three months by 18.3 percent. However, 62 per cent of this increase comes from group tours, a part of the business that is normally not as time-consuming as individual sales. He has therefore decided not to increase his staff. He has granted a 10 per cent salary increase, since he is probably straining his staff to a maximum point of efficiency, and he may consider hiring an additional employee in the second quarter.

Occupancy: He has no reason to expect this cost to increase except for a few dollars for the traditional midnight oil.

Advertising and Promotion: The agent already was spending a high proportion of his advertising budget to promote group tours during these traditionally unprofitable months. The decision to increase this budget is part of his effort to increase tour profits and therefore distribute business more evenly over this 3-month period.

Office Supplies and Equipment: This increase is directly proportionate to increased volume.

Telephone and Telegraph: Normally this expense increases by almost the same percentage as business. However, because of the decreased need for long distance tolls to tour operators and hotels, our agent has shown only a 5 per cent increase.

Education: Remains the same since there is no increase in staff.

Postage and Miscellaneous: Increase is in approximately the same proportion as business.

In our example of budgeting we find an agent who has realistically budgeted an 18.3 per cent increase in gross earnings and a whopping 62.3 per cent increase in net profits! This is not too infrequent an example. The agent has accomplished this by avoiding an additional employee until such a time when his increased sales will warrant this additional expense without a resulting loss in net profit.

The percentages are not pertinent to any particular agency. The developing of a budget and the continued comparing of the budget (yes, continued changing of the budget if circumstances warrant) to the

110

actual results is not only pertinent but imperative if your business is to be profitable.

Cash Flow and Its Use

According to Prentice-Hall *Encyclopedic Dictionary of Business Finance*, the words "cash flow" mean "the change in the cash account in a given period." It further states, "The increase or decrease of cash during the period is accounted for by analyzing the sources and applications of cash."

This statement is a little bookish for a travel agency, so let's approach the definition of "cash flow" in agents' terms. All "cash flow" amounts to is the day by day knowledge of your cash position and its relationship to future budgeted expenditures.

A few years ago a prominent travel agent declared bankruptcy. His income had always been quite high, his personal cost of living reasonable, and yet he went bankrupt. The agent had booked a very large pilgrimage to the Holy Land. His potential profit was $30-40,000 and his cash position had been favorable. Further, he had already invested about $20,000 in cash in the program which would be returned along with his profit. He considered this a good time to expand his operation and leased a larger office, redecorated, added two new staff members and consequently advertised more to keep them busy. Then, due to circumstances beyond his and the group's control, the tour had to be cancelled. He not only lost his $20,000 investment but he also could no longer afford expansion. The result, of course, was bankruptcy. He didn't own the money he was spending. He did not know his cash position. A lesson in cash flow could have saved him and his agency.

The basic requirements in your office are a monthly P & L Statement, a budget, a monthly list of payables and receivables, and an aging report on receivables no less than once per month and preferably every week or two. A monthly balance sheet is also important.

Cash flow is certainly more than knowing your gross sales or gross commissions and expenses. It is also much more than knowing how much money is in the bank. You may have a large bank balance, as was the case of our bankrupt agent in the previous example, but none of the money belongs to you. If you are continually in debt to the bank to cover receivables, you had better stop and look at your cash flow. After all, your debtors are not immune to business failure.

Here is the way we look at our cash flow on a monthly basis using fictitious figures:

CASH PROVIDED BY:

Commissions	$7,500.00
Sale of related items	75.00
Interest earned	300.00
Miscellaneous	25.00
Total	$7,900.00

CASH APPLIED TO:

Operating expenses	$6,400.00
Fixtures and equipment (deprc.)	700.00
Interest	100.00
Miscellaneous	50.00
Total	$7,250.00
INCREASE IN CASH	$650.00

Yes, cash flow is the knowledge of the money you have, where it is, how fast it is coming in, and when it is to be used. Keep a monthly record of your cash flow and you will soon find that it is one more valuable tool in the financial management of your agency.

Service Charges

In the past few years, there has been a growing feeling in the retail travel agency industry in favor of service charges. For years, the large retail travel chains and some smaller agencies have been charging T & T (telephone and telegraph), many times without the prior knowledge of

112

the client. This is certainly a **BONA FIDE** charge to present to your client, yet many agents are afraid the client will rebel and go elsewhere with his business. This fear is unwarranted provided your client is told in advance that he is expected to pay for all long distance tolls and other unusual communication charges. Many agents even ask the client's permission to charge these T & T charges directly to the client's home or office telephone account. This generally receives a quick O.K., and not only is the cost of the call saved, but all necessary bookkeeping and collection of this expense is eliminated.

Service charges are necessary under many circumstances, but your client should be completely aware of the way your "service charge" policy affects his pocketbook.

What are service charges? They can be the monies paid for the services of a professional, such as a doctor, attorney or C.P.A. As much as many agents would enjoy being identified with these and other professions, it appears that few would survive if they depended solely on professional fees.

The fees that we refer to are those charged for hotel reservations, rail tickets, non-commissionable transactions, delivery charges, etc. Each agent prior to formulating a policy on service charges must decide what the underlying reason is for wanting service charges in the first place.

1. Is it in order to discourage business not wanted, i.e., do you want to charge for rail tickets in order to chase your client to your competitor or directly to the railroad?

2. Are you trying to establish an image of a specific type of agent? Do you discourage domestic tickets in order to develop a following of international travelers?

3. Have you established service charges in order to bolster your profit picture? Are you charging for unprofitable business and still encouraging the public to come to you for these services?

If either of the first two reasons is true, perhaps you might pick a figure out of a hat and call that your service charge, and the higher the better, for your primary purpose is then to discourage these transactions. This charge can't be equated in any manner to the professional's fee, because you are discouraging rather than encouraging business.

However, if you choose the latter reason, you must determine your charges on a businesslike basis. Let's use some fictitious figures again. You may decide, after reviewing your past years P & L Statement, that you must earn $5,000 more net profit based on the same volume, commissions and expenses. You then review all of the services you perform at a loss and decide which services deserve further remuneration.

Look first at your telephone and telegraph charges. In this case you may find that you could have charged $2,000 to your clients that in the previous year you paid yourself. Make the decision to begin charging for T & T and earn that extra $2,000.

Next examine the number of hotel reservations and non-commissionable auto rentals made without charge to your customers. If there were 800 such transactions last year, determine a charge for the coming year. A $3 service charge is generally considered a minimum amount and many agents feel quite comfortable with a $5 service charge. Even at $3 you have a return of $2,400.

One-way rail and bus tickets, or roundtrip non RTPA rail, can earn from $3 to $5 transmittal charge per ticket. Pullman accommodations can also be included in this category. If you have one hundred such transactions per year, this adds up to $500. There are other irritating free services many agents perform — *bon voyage* gifts purchased by friends of clients, tickets for plays and theatres, and many others that can draw a $1 to $5 charge per transaction. It is possible to add another $1,100 to your total. You should then be able to budget $6,000 or so more income for your next fiscal year. If 15 to 20 per cent of your clients decide they do not wish to pay for these services, you still have the $5,000 extra profit that is so important.

We recommend that you must make steps toward becoming a "professional" or at least a well-trained businessman, a merchant who decides his own mark-up (service charges) and does so with two end results in mind:

1. To remain in competition in the marketplace.
2. To operate at a satisfactory net profit.

Being competitive, alone, is not enough, for without profit there will be no business to remain competitive. When choosing between being

114

competitive and charging service charges that give you an opportunity to show a profit, choose the latter and remember that hundreds of retailers before you charged higher prices and still profited as a result of better service. The public is willing to pay for what it receives. If your service is superior, your prices do not have to be competitive.

Two important warnings in regard to service charges must be kept in mind when you formulate your policy:

1. Your sales agency agreement presently prohibits service charges on air reservations, tickets, cancellations and refunds, or any other service which is an integral part of air transportation.

2. Any service charge policy must be made clear to your customers prior to the time they assume the responsibility of paying that charge. I recommend that you post all service charges in a conspicuous place in your waiting room or sales areas, and secondly, that you have a specific written statement of your policies available to give to your clients prior to their commitment to pay for your services.

Long Range Planning

Prior to every year's budgeting plan for a fiscal year five years in the future. If you find this process helpful, you may want to try the same planning for ten years in the future.

Generally speaking, your travel agency's image is formed by the kind of trips sold in the past. Any time you wish to change that image, the past can become your greatest obstacle. You can't change the past, and you can't change the future unless you are willing to do so gradually and with well conceived planning.

What should your travel agency look like in five years? First, consider what the traveler is going to want in five years. Is he going to be traveling in large groups as the trend appears today? Is it possible that today's large groups are only an introduction to travel, and in five years participants will start seeking out new continents on their own? Are FITs, with the high cost of personal service, a product of the past? Will the U. S. traveler join the European trend of spending two weeks at one resort, using charters to get there? Will the lack of "individuality" on some tours today "turn off" tomorrow's traveler on groups, or even to travel itself? Will the three-day holiday plan create a new trend in destinations or transportation? Will the trend towards longer vacations mean a return to the six-to-eight week all inclusive tour? What will today's 21-year-old want from travel when he is 26 or 31? How will the youth of tomorrow vary from today's "independent" youth? Present trends indicate high incidence of travel for high school students. How young will tomorrow's traveler be?

We've only scratched the surface with questions you can ask yourself when planning on a long range basis. Besides wanting to know what the industry will look like, you will want to decide which elements of the public you desire to attract to your office.

There are questions pertaining to conditions other than the travel market that are also important. How will automation affect your operation in five or ten years? Will a combination of credit cards and automated ticketing eliminate commercial business? Will air buses eliminate the need for a ticket? Will the products you have to sell determine the patronage you receive? Or, will your knowledge and ability serve to determine that patronage? Will automation replace the wholesaler of hotel packages? If so, who will become the operator of tours, the retailer or the wholesaler?

Yes, there are many more questions than accepted answers. Make your own guesses, then plan your business to reflect the travel community as you see it in five or ten years. There are many directions your business can go. Some of these are:

1. The same size business, but more profitable. This may be your direction. If it is, you'll want to plan each year in such a manner as to eliminate your low yield business and add business that is high yield. You may have to resign accounts from year to year, or charge a service fee as previously discussed.

2. You may wish to be a large supermarket of travel. If you do, you'll want to specialize in the type of travel that you believe will exist in five to ten years. You'll want to add staff that has permanence, and you'll want to see that their training reflects the needs of tomorrow's traveler. For the agent who wants to become big, long range planning is essential. You will have to avoid the pitfalls of growing large. Pitfalls such as bookkeeping systems that make a slave of you, forms and systems left over from your small volume days that create unnecessary

work, over-emphasis on some low commission business, or over-emphasis on seasonal promotions that make your sales charts look like a profile of the Alps.

In order to develop size and profit simultaneously, each year must be planned well in advance, and a five to ten year plan can give you an opportunity to judge your results.

3. Possibly you may wish to go the branch route. Many agents have found that carefully located branches can be profitable. First, one must consider the duplicated cost of rental, equipment and so on. It takes very efficient staffs to show greater profit from branches than would be shown in one large office. So, if you want to branch out, you'll have to start shopping for your branch locations well in advance, and most carefully. At the same time, you will probably have a different personnel policy from your competitors. Your personnel programs will be based on developing a top grade sales and office manager, not just a travel salesman.

Whether you think your five to ten year future holds mergers, development of group business, commercial accounts, package sales, FITs, or a reversion to "space-on-deck" sales, your primary responsibility as a manager or owner is to anticipate those trends well in advance and build your business to profit from these trends and opportunities.

Chapter 6

Automation and the Future

by

Richard F. Cook

The entire subject of automation can be viewed as either a threat to the travel agent, or as the one vehicle that can wage the travel agent's battle against inflated operating costs. In fact, both are true. Which viewpoint applies to each individual agency depends upon the agent's willingness to adjust to automation.

Look to the Future

It is my firm belief that one-half of the agency industry will be automated in the areas of reservations and bookkeeping by 1976. I would also venture to state that all those agents who wish to remain competitive will be automated by 1980. There will be, however, a group of agents (possibly as high as 30 per cent) who will find automation too costly and therefore be forced to find an economical way of sharing these costs with other agents.

Many theorists predict automated equipment will soon have the capacity not only to confirm air reservations, but after accepting a credit card, will identify the holder of same, compute fares, issue airline tickets, boarding passes, baggage tags and even go so far as to give the client a choice of hotels at his destination and confirm his selection. Some observers go further and envision the baggage being transferred to the hotel at the destination by the airline. To deny these probabilities would serve only to ignore the inevitable. In fact, I believe that within 10 years, some of these innovations will be as commonplace as the *Quick Reference Edition* of the OAG is today.

Computer Limitations

How will automation with its super efficiency affect the role of the travel agent in the future? First, consider the fact that it is impossible to build a computer that has imagination. Nor is it possible to send the computer off to Paris to inspect a dozen or so hotels and sample the nightlife and restaurants; nor can the computer return to the office and knowledgeably counsel the client, interpreting his desires in travel and set up a personalized trip, based on expertise. We will not see a computer that can be programmed to answer the myriad questions regarding clothing, weather, entertainment, visas, health requirements, special events and other subjects that arise daily in the average agency.

The agent will definitely play an important role in the Computer Age, particularly in the case of the first time traveler, the vacationing tourist and the traveler visiting a new destination, as well as those belonging to specially promoted groups. All of these types of travelers will continue to seek the advice of imaginative and knowledgeable agents.

Computer Advantages and Uses

Yet, at the same time, this personal service will not suffice in the '70s without the facility of almost instant reservation and ticketing service. When it takes an agent weeks to obtain a hotel room in Paris, compared to seconds when requested through a computer, then personal attention will be equated against speed by many of your clients, for you deal with an impatient public. Speed will frequently be the victor.

Are hotel reservations the only reason the travel agent must become automated? Don't forget your present high cost of doing business. Also take a look at the comparative service between your office and your largest principal, the airline. A passenger can today call the airline and, through automation, receive an immediate confirmation and alternate availability if desired. He can hang up the phone, turn to his family and announce their exact vacation plans, including hotel reservations and tours, in many instances.

What happens when that same passenger calls the travel agent? It would be an exceptional agent who could obtain air and hotel space while the passenger is still on the telephone. In fact, as you encounter unavailable flights and hotels, it is likely that more than one return telephone call will be necessary, not to mention the delay in time between the passenger's original request and final confirmation.

Until a parity can be reached in the time it takes to confirm a reservation, the travel agent can not fulfill his complete responsibility to his principal and to the traveling public. Fortunately, the service rendered in the area of peripheral knowledge (advice on hotels, tours, health, clothing, travel documents, etc.) has enabled the travel agent to become increasingly important as a counselor to the vacation-bound public.

The travel agent will find not only a way of competing (automation plus personal service) for the discretionary vacation dollar, but, more than likely, he will be the forerunner in the tremendous growth of vacation travel. How about the travel agent who depends, to varying degrees, on commercial business for his livelihood? Will this part of his business still exist in the future?

This question has been raised because the airlines are already experimenting with ticketing machines that accept credit cards as payment. My first answer is directed to the agent whose commercial accounts are a minority part of his volume. To this agent, I'd say don't take a chance. Start promoting more vacation travel and see to it that your public image is primarily that of a vacation planner. You do not have to surrender your commercial business, but you should be continually developing new vacation business in the event of eventual loss of your commercial accounts.

For the few travel agents who have enjoyed success primarily in the commercial field, I have a different answer. You will spend a great deal of your time in the future working closely with automation. Not only automated reservations, as I shall describe, but with other forms of automation as well. You are going to be constantly challenged to come up with systems that will assist your accounts more than those systems offered your customers directly by other purveyors of travel and transportation services.

Key is Repetition

Any time the same function in your office is performed more than one time, that function is a target for automation. If the same letter is written to several clients, that letter could be automated. Internal bookkeeping shows an obvious need for automation. Here is a list of some of the internal agency functions that can be automated:

1. Sales, confirmations and other letters
2. Itineraries and vouchers
3. Bookkeeping
4. Airline reports
5. Management information
6. Hotel, tour and auto rental requests
7. Air reservations
8. Computation of fares
9. Air tickets issuance
10. Retrieval of filed information.

The list is probably endless. While the travel agent deals with a variety of customers and their individual problems, the basic information desired remains the same and is re-used constantly. This fact makes the travel industry a prime target for automation.

Letter Writing: Secretarial wages have increased dramatically in the past few years, while the volume of work processed by most secretaries has been constant. This is due to the fact that the maximum typing speed has not appreciably changed. In the past decade a great many new business machines have been introduced that can speed the completion of letters when specific paragraphs are frequently repeated

122

and filed in such as way as to make them available to the typist. When the pre-prepared tape is fed to the typewriter, it proceeds to complete the work at approximately 200 to 250 words per minute. The most modern equipment allows for the insertion of special information (such as the name of the person you are addressing) in the middle of the tape.

The key to making this kind of equipment work for you is to be fully aware of everything it can do and then take the time to program the equipment into your operation.

A list of the variety of work that can best be produced by typewriters with tape drive capabilities follows:

1. Personalized sales letters
2. Personalized invitations
3. Welcome-home letters
4. Letters accompanying final credentials
5. Thank you — acknowledging deposits
6. Paragraphs within letters detailing visa, health, weather and clothing information
8. Answers to inquiries.

Once again this list can be endless and probably will be as your imagination runs wild. At any rate, analyze the cost of labor presently expended on these functions and equate the possible savings against the cost of automated typing equipment. Most manufacturers of electric typewriters have a line of this kind of equipment.

Itineraries: In the event that a large number of individualized itineraries are prepared in your office, it may pay for you to review the paragraphs or statements that are continually repeated. They also can be put on tape and inserted in itineraries as they are prepared. The same equipment mentioned above will do the job.

Bookkeeping, Air Reports, and Management Information: This book carries a full chapter on "Profit Planning through Correct Accounting Practices." The full subject deserves further attention as it is related to automation. When one document must be used to develop two or more different reports or bits of information, automation of these reports deserves study. For example: many agents today are preparing air reports from auditor's coupons and then turning around and using the same coupons to develop their internal bookkeeping system. There is no reason that both steps can not be accomplished simultaneously. While there are expensive accounting machines and computers that can be programmed to accomplish both tasks at once, don't forget that a piece of carbon paper might do much the same thing.

In the profit planning chapter, the use of management information in the travel business was discussed. The modern agent uses his financial information in three ways: air reports, bookkeeping, and management information. As all three reports come from the same basic information, we now have a candidate for automated equipment with greater capacity than the sheet of carbon paper.

Tailoring Computers to the Job

Several dozen travel agents have already spent thousands of dollars for programs to develop automated accounting through the use of computers. As a general rule, these systems have been designed to answer one agent's problems and are not universally accepted. A system that is designed for an agent who handles many group tour bookings is not necessarily good for the agent who specializes in point to point travel. A system that is deisgned for an agent who has accounts receivable problems is over-designed for the agent who does not extend credit.

At the present time, several companies are hard at work developing a computerized system that will answer most agents' problems. This will be a modular system. The agent will be able to purchase a simplified system of accounting and add to it the modules of his choice — air reports, accounts receivable aging, Profit and Loss Statements, and management information.

Before a travel agent can determine which system or which modules to buy, he must be fully aware of his present internal cost of these functions. No one expects a computerized system to eliminate the accountant who does your tax work and prepares balance sheets and audits. A good internal time study of the amount of time and corresponding salaries presently being expended in the area of bookkeeping, air reports, etc., will provide the financial information that will be needed tomorrow in order to make a decision as to whether you should automate these functions.

Automated Reservations

This discussion of computerized reservations could be a complicated thesis. Instead, the subject will be discussed in layman's terms and, for this purpose, definitions of the unavoidable computer or communication terminology follow:

Computer: While the computer is one of man's most advanced forms of technology, for our purposes it is simply a library of stored information. With almost unbelievable speed the computer can retrieve this stored information and display it in a logical manner. In addition to the storage and retrieval of information, computers can serve as adding machines or calculators. (This applies to the travel agent's bookkeeping problems.)

For hotel and air reservations the storage of information can take two basic forms: "Negative Availability" means the space is always available until a "sold out" message is received and stored by the computer; "Positive Availability" means an actual inventory of rooms

125

or seats is available in the computer until such a time as that inventory has been exhausted.

Terminal: For the travel agent's purposes, this is the physical equipment that allows conversation between the computer and the interested party. It allows an individual to request information or have information sent in his behalf and it receives the response. There are several types of terminals which may eventually be used in the agent's office.

Hard Copy Terminal: The most frequently used terminal has a typewriter appearance. In addition to the normal keys, the terminal will have special keys that apply to the functions the terminal is to perform. The hard copy terminal has a platen similar to the typewriter's which is used to receive information from the computer printed, or "typed," on roll-fed paper.

Cathode Ray Tube (CRT): This equipment resembles a television screen. The screen is used instead of the hard copy terminal to list flight schedules and/or availability. It is still necessary to use a keyboard to transmit the reserve message, but the CRT flashes the schedules on a screen in fractions of a second, while the printer takes longer to reply, typing out the same information. At the present time, CRT for use in an agent's office will cost $100 to $150 per month more than the hard copy terminal.

Receive Only Printer: This looks like a typewriter without a keyboard. It is used to receive printed hard copy when a CRT is used, or when no terminal is available in the agent's office.

Program: This is the actual design of the material stored in the memory units of the computer. The program controls the information that can be accepted by the computer and is responsible for the information that is returned.

Passenger Name Record: The passenger's name and full itinerary is called the Passenger Name Record (PNR).

Interface: The technology of connecting entirely separate computer systems so that they can communicate with each other. For example, an airline computer used primarily for airline reservations could be interfaced with a hotel reservations computer. The airline computer would then tap the storage of hotel rooms from the hotel computer and receive confirmation.

126

Flight Segment Availability: The most complete system of airline reservations will confirm space on a flight segment basis. This means that the computer will store each leg of a New York-Honolulu-Tokyo-Hong Kong flight. No matter whether New York-Tokyo or Honolulu-Hong Kong is requested, the computer will determine the availability of each leg of space that makes up the requested flight segment and then confirm or deny confirmation.

Flight Number Availability: Due to lack of storage capacity, many computers (particularly when dealing with interline space) will confirm only by flight number. Using the above example of a New York-Tokyo flight, if it were sold out on the New York-Honolulu leg, then all flight segments would also be closed for sale.

Almost all airline systems today are off-shoots of American's Sabre System and Pan American's Panamac. A description of both systems follows.

Panamac

The Panamac System allows for the sale of seats on most of the world's air carriers, as well as on Pan Am. Carriers other than Pan Am make their space available on either a free sale basis or a negative availability basis, negative availability meaning that Pan Am is free to sell up to four seats on a given flight, confirm to the requesting party and then transmit the passenger name(s) to the carrier whose seats have been sold. Only when the carrier advises Pan Am that a specific flight is sold out, does this flight become unavailable in Pan Am's records.

In addition to airline seats, Pan Am makes hotel space, auto rentals and tours available to agents calling the Panamac operator. These are also available on a free sale or negative availability basis.

When a travel agent calls a Panamac operator, here is what happens. First, the travel agent may ask for one of the following options:
1. To request a specific flight
2. To request available flights around a desired time
3. To request a list of flight schedules around a desired time

While the order of request is unimportant to Pan Am, this is not true of some other systems. Therefore, it is good business for the travel agent to keep his reservation records and to make his request in the following order: AIRLINE, FLIGHT NUMBER, CLASS OF SERVICE, DATE, MONTH, ORIGIN, DESTINATION, NUMBER OF PASSENGERS.

A standard request would be: Requesting PA flight 2, first class, 15 January, New York to London, for a party of two.

Requesting tours: Pan Am has included in its availability all tours operated by major tour operators in conjunction with Pan Am. These are also available through Panamac. Reservations will be confirmed over the telephone, and either a deposit or tour order may be sent directly to the tour operator.

Pan Am works on a flight segment basis for its own flights, but works on a flight number basis on those flights of other carriers. In the event your Panamac operator is not able to confirm a flight on another carrier, it may be still available through the other carrier's own reservation office and Pan Am will query the second carrier directly.

In the event you need assistance with fare construction, the Panamac operator will forward your request to a rate desk. The Panamac operator is directed to keep a close follow-up on the answers to fare requests.

Sabre System

American Airlines Sabre System of reservations was the first major airline system to be made available to travel agents for use in the agent's office.

Travel agents renting these sets pay $225 per month for the Sabre terminal. This is a typewriter-like keyboard terminal, which gives unlimited access to almost all domestic flight availability on a *flight number* basis. Flight segment availability can be obtained for American Airlines flights only. If one segment of any other carrier's flight number is on request, all segments will be shown as on request. In this event, the Sabre set user must call the airline in question to ascertain if the desired flight segment is available.

The Sabre set is programmed to retrieve the Passenger Name Record on request of the operator. For the high volume travel agency this means that it is no longer necessary to retain the complete record of each passenger. All you need is the name and first flight segment information.

128

It is possible to receive your hard copy print-out in two copies. Several agents keep one copy for their permanent file and attach another copy to the passenger's ticket. Today's experienced air travelers feel more at ease with a computer confirmation than they do with an oral confirmation. Many agents have used this fact and the hard copy print-out as a major marketing tool.

If the travel agent wishes to use the Sabre set for international reservations, he may do so for an additional cost of $25 per month. An agent who uses Sabre will be advised periodically of all changes in his passengers' flight schedules as announced by the carriers.

Sabre can be used as a "teletype" machine to convey messages to the American Airlines reservation center. Operators at American can take requests for special meal service, wheelchair service, VIP assistance, seat selection and even hotel requests, in the case of the Flagship Hotels.

Should you have a Sabre set in your office? Obviously, American is interested in placing the sets in only those offices which have sufficient volume with a high incidence of American Airline flights. It is further true that the computers of American will only be able to service a small percentage of all the travel agents. However, these facts aside, the final judgment must be made by comparing cost versus savings. The final subject of this chapter will deal with this question of costs.

A Common Airline Reservation System

As early as 1967 a committee of airline experts in automation decided that no one airline could be expected to become the supplier of automated reservation equipment to the travel agency industry. It was further decided that if all airlines were to enter into competitive placement of equipment in agents' offices, that the profusion of terminals and the resulting cost to agents and airlines would be prohibitive. This committee then set out to develop a system that could be used by all travel agents to obtain available space from all domestic airlines.

The technical committee developed a series of specifications that were to be met by a future supplier for the "common system." Chosen from these three was a company named AtarCSI, commonly called ATAR. ATAR was to sign a contract with ATC as provider of the system if it were able to obtain contracts from ten or more air carriers who were responsible for over 50 per cent of the domestic passenger miles. ATAR completed its responsibility by signing Alaska, Continental, Delta, Eastern, Mohawk, National, Northeast, Northwest, Trans World, United and Western. These airlines represent approximately 75 per cent of the available passenger miles in the United States.

The CAB has called for an evidentiary hearing on the ATAR/ATC agreement. Since a hearing of this type generally takes from 12 to 18 months or longer, it is unlikely that ATAR or any other company undertaking this large financial commitment can sustain this lengthy delay.

It appears, then, that if a "common" supplier is to be found, it will be the result of competition in the marketplace. Because of the present open competition and confusion in the area of automated reservations, a list follows of the technical features that the individual agent should look for when signing a contract for an automated reservation system.

1. Travel Agency Oriented: Is the system designed for use by the travel agent, or is the agency system a by-product of other system uses? It is inconceivable that any system designed for uses other than the travel agents' will bring maximum efficiency to the agent. The agent who adopts an automated system must be assured of continuous service.

2. IBM-PARS System: It appears that any successful agency system will be a result of an adaptation of the IBM-PARS system. Several airlines attempted to use other systems designed specifically for them, and most, if not all, have changed to IBM. At this stage, it appears that this system is the only answer to agency automation.

3. Communication Lines: The system will attract the maximum number of agents if it is developed in two stages related to the speed of communications. High speed lines will be necessary to serve the high-volume or large population area agents. A slower speed line will most economically serve the agent in remote locations.

4. Flight Space Availability: The computer must be able to store all flight segments for all major domestic and international carriers, preferably on a negative availability system. If a flight is sold out,

alternate available flights should be displayed. It would also be helpful if agents could request a display of all available flights.

5. Terminals: The terminals should have a typewriter or similar keyboard for ease of training. Most agents will find hard copy print-outs sufficient for their needs. The extremely high-volume agent may require cathode ray or similar display equipment.

6. Interface: There is no question that a system that is capable of direct request to the airlines' central computer through an interface technique would be far superior to one having negative availability in a separate computer. The capacity of airline computers may prevent this happening even if the airlines are willing to make their entire inventory available.

7. Cost: This important factor is discussed in full at the end of the chapter. However, those agencies having a very large air volume should consider the installation of more than one terminal. No terminal can be expected to handle more than approximately $600,000 in air reservations. Larger volume agents should study their entire needs before ordering. One terminal that can't do the full job is probably worse than no automation at all.

8. Passenger Name Record Retrieval: Some systems are designed to retrieve entire passenger transactions from the computer. Normally, this is intended to relieve the booking agent of keeping passenger records. For travel agents who book more than point-to-point travel, this record of passenger name, hotels, sightseeing, etc., will probably still be maintained. Therefore, there exists little need for PNR retrieval for this type of agency, unless ticket issuance by computer becomes a reality. When the computer is used to trigger automated ticket issuance, it will have to be programmed to store and retrieve all passenger name records.

9. Ancillary Services: While automated reservations alone would be a giant step for the travel agent, it is conceivable that bookkeeping, air reports, management records, hotel and auto reservations, tour reservations and other services may be incorporated into a future system. Each agent should study his agency's needs and select the system that best complies.

Hotel Reservation Systems

The Telemax System

Telemax, the first of the independent automated reservation systems, has developed a diversified approach to the reservation business. The heart of its business in the early stages was to provide "in house" reservation facilities for chain motel firms and auto rental companies. Quality Courts was one of the early users of the system. Terminals were placed in their motels and used to reserve space from one motel to the next. The same concept was used for National Car Rental. Best Western, Marriott and Budget Rent-a-Car are more recent additions to the Telemax Reservation System.

The next step was to connect these facilities with the travel agent. Over 100 sets were placed in agencies, allowing these agents to reserve space in any subscribing properties or car rental firms. Telemax then entered into agreement with American Airlines, Frontier and ten international carriers to make flight reservations available to agents using the Telemax terminal.

At the present time the Telemax terminals consist of:
1. CRT unit and printer
2. Hard copy terminal
3. Receive only printer

Unlike other systems the receive only printer is designed to accept confirmation for reservations made through Telemax's System 800. The System 800 is designed for the use of both hotels and travel agents who can not economically support the cost of the other terminals. By using the toll-free WATS system, an agent can call the Telemax computer center in Omaha, Nebraska. He will be connected with a Telemax operator who can request airline, hotel, motel or car rental availability on Telemax's high speed CRT terminal. Within seconds confirmation can be given orally to the travel agent. For those who desire to install the printer unit, hard copy confirmation can also be received in seconds. Agents without the printer can request hard copy by mail.

This equipment should soon be available at costs ranging from approximately $75 for the printer, and up to $250 for both printer and CRT unit.

132

American Express Reservation Service   "Space Bank"

The American Express Reservation System, known as the "Space Bank," serves such companies as Ramada Inns, Western International Hotels and Hyatt House Motels. Hundreds of thousands of other chain and independent hotel rooms, as well as Hertz and Avis car rentals, are offered to the public and to travel agents through the use of the Space Bank.

Travel agents make their reservations by using the toll-free WATS service which connects them with the American Express Reservation Service in Memphis, Tennessee. As in the Telemax system, oral confirmation is given in seconds. A hard copy confirmation will be mailed to the agent if he requests it. No travel agency terminal set is offered at this time.

In addition to the wide variety of hotels and car rentals, American Express Hawaii tours can be reserved through the Space Bank and more tours can be expected to be available in the future. American Express also has an agreement with one international carrier and can be expected to eventually compete in the air reservation field.

International Reservation Corporation (IRC)

Like some of the other hotel reservation systems, IRC had its beginnings with "in house" reservation services for Howard Johnson Motels, Royal Inns and the Downtowner Hotels. In addition, IRC has an agreement with the American Automobile Association to provide reservation services between AAA offices on one hand and AAA approved and contraced hotels and motels on the other. Hertz auto rentals are also obtainable through IRC.

Four centralized reservation centers service the travel agent through WATS lines. Hard copy is sent to the agent if reservations are received prior to one week in advance. Hotels are advised of reservations through terminals installed in the hotels, or by telephone and mail if they do not have a terminal. There is no charge to the travel agent for using the IRC reservation services and commissions are paid to the agent by those hotels with commission policies.

Time will surely bring modifications; perhaps these companies described will not be affected. but certainly changes will be made in the basic structure of some systems. It is inconceivable that four systems can serve this vast industry in what appears to be three or four different ways. One of the companies now charges the hotel a straight 5 per cent for all reservations (and insists upon the agent's 10 per cent protection), in addition to a possible 4 per cent credit card expense. This makes the hotel cost of credit card, agent and computer reservation service to come out to 19 per cent! Another company receives a straight 10 per cent of every reservation, direct or through an agent. Two of the companies levy a monthly charge (based on the number of rooms) on the hotel and charge an additional amount for every room used. This latter example also protects the agent's commission.

Up to this point, we have not discussed the facilities of the automated hotel reservation systems to handle requests for properties located outside the United States. Due to rapid advances in technology and competitive pressures, it is difficult to ascertain which firm will be serving what new areas within a month, a year, or ever.

Generally speaking, at the present time most hotels in Hawaii and some in Mexico are available through one of more of the systems. The Orient and South Pacific are quite well covered by the American Express Space Bank. Hotels in Europe are partially covered by the IRC system. Intercontinental Hotels can be reserved through Panamac.

All of these companies provide a manual of the hotels they service, which is free to travel agents. It would pay the agent to keep these manuals handy, and it would also be wise to keep a central reference guide as to who represents which property. This can be accomplished by coding your favorite hotel guide. As new areas are introduced, you will want to take advantage of the reduced communication costs and make use of these various reservation services.

It is interesting to note that insiders estimate that well over 50 per cent of the hotels are duplicated from one system to the other.

It is also interesting to observe that few, if any, of these systems are designed to recommend specific hotels. They will check the availability of your desired hotel, or they will check which hotels in a specific city are available and then let you select your property. A travel agent with either the personal knowledge of hotels or excellent reference material should be able to please clients on a more consistent basis than the reservation systems dealing direct, if the agent can match the speed and convenience of the WATS call and rapid computerized confirmation.

It is obvious what would happen if interfacing were not possible between a common airline reservation system and the hotel systems. We would have to have several terminals in each office or one company would end up handling all hotels. Instead, the travel agent should eventually have the choice of several terminals, all of which are interfaced with several other reservations systems.

I have stated earlier that some agents will not be financially able to participate in automation as I have described here. What will be their alternative? We have already seen a move in the direction of servicing these agents — American Express, IRC, and Telemax have all established their computer centers connected by WATS lines, enabling the agent, for the price of a local call, to request and receive immediate confirmation on desired hotel space. If a hard copy confirmation is also required, it will be mailed to the agent.

Evaluating Automation Expense and Feasibility

Every travel agent should make maximum use of automation as long as economics, sufficient additional sales, or both result. The decision facing the agent will be to choose a system for his office which provides the greatest reservation capacity (airline, hotel, tour, car rental) at the most economical price. He will also have to consider the ease of operation, repair facilities and the long range interests of each company.

It appears in the early stages that the WATS line systems for hotel and car rental reservations for the price of one local call will replace the need for multiple local and occasional long distance calls to gain the same result. As long as the service can be kept consistently fast, it appears that the WATS system can also replace the high cost of mail requests to hotels.

The real question seems to be in the area of airline reservations. What volume of air reservations is necessary in order to effect economies through the rental of terminal equipment for use in your office? The answer to this varies, and consideration should be given to the following factors:

1. The agent who pays toll charges (including nominal long distance charges) for telephone service to air carriers, will be able to show a saving quicker than those agents who do not pay toll calls.

2. How much time do reservation personnel spend "holding" on the phone, and how effectively do they make use of this "holding" time?

3. Can one or two operators be trained to use the terminal equipment and be stationed in such a way as to avoid confusion in gaining access to the reservation equipment?

4. Have you had reasonably good experience in holding your staff? Turnover in personnel can be costly as you train staff to use automated equipment.

5. Through advertising and public relations promotions, can the volume of profitable sales be increased with the use of computerized reservations on your premises?

6. How much is it worth to build the additional good will that will result from faster confirmation to your clients?

These are just a few of the questions to ask yourself.

You may find three, or even more, salesmen on your doorstep in the next year who will be trying to sell you a plan to lease their terminal and go on-line. How can you determine which system will be best for you? Don't take the chance that you might be led to drowning in the River Weser by a modern Pied Piper. Instead, be prepared with facts and figures relating to the monies you can save through automation.

The Touche, Ross, Bailey, and Smart Cost Study is a good place to start. Touche completed work sampling studies in over 400 agencies to determine the cost of selling domestic air tickets. I have used these figures and adjusted them slightly to reflect the increased cost of a domestic ticket and the inflationary cost of personnel. I have also eliminated the listing of many of the costs that will not change with the introduction of automation as we know it today.

The following figures are the approximate costs of direct labor in the selling of a domestic ticket (average of $100 per ticket):

Customer Contacts
Telephone	$ .59
Face to face	.40
Letters	.03

Making Reservations

Telephone	.46
Direct access	.03
Itinerary preparation	.22
Total direct labor costs pertaining to reservations and itinerary	$1.73

The cost of the time spent on the telephone, both with the airline and your customer, should be substantially reduced. My estimate is from 20 to 25 per cent, or at least 35¢ per ticket. In addition, there is a direct saving of telephone charges. My estimate is a minimum of two calls per customer. Depending upon your local telephone charges, this saving could vary from 10¢ to 30¢. For this example I will use a saving of 15¢ per ticket. Therefore, our entire saving for each domestic air ticket is 50¢. In order to lease a piece of equipment costing $225 per month for domestic air only, a volume of 450 tickets, or a dollar volume of $45,000 per month, must be achieved. Domestic reservation equipment costing $110 will require 220 tickets, or $22,000, in domestic air sales per month.

The cost of reserving and itinerizing international flights is not projected. I would estimate the cost of reserving, and consequently the saving through automation, to be approximately double that of domestic air, let's say $1 saving per ticket.

Hotel systems and the eventual saving to travel agents depend greatly upon the system the agent has been using in the past. If you have been absorbing long distance telephone calls or writing letters, either a hotel terminal or the use of the WATS systems will save money on very little volume. On the other hand, if you are presently using the WATS systems, you will find that your volume of hotel reservations will have to be very high (possibly as high as air reservations) in order to replace the WATS system with a terminal set.

If both hotel reservations and most or all air reservations can be obtained through the use of one terminal, your volume may not have to be quite as high as previously mentioned.

As bookkeeping and other services are added to the system, less volume will be required to "break even."

The term "break even" has been used because that is all that has been accomplished in our calculations up to this point. The savings shown here have been a result primarily from the saving of your employees' time. If your employees do not use this time to sell more travel, you haven't broken even. In fact, you have lost almost the entire cost of automation. This is one of the reasons I strongly suggested, in the "Profit Planning Through Correct Accounting Practices" chapter of this book, that you keep accurate records of your employees' contributions to your earnings. This contribution must increase by a total amount greater than the cost of automation (the leasing of a terminal), or all has been lost.

This is the decade of automation for the travel agent. By 1976, we should experience a degree of progress resulting in cutting the cost factor of making an airline reservation by a reasonable margin, and the cost of completing a hotel reservation by an even greater percentage. We should have tour availability offered, as well. In some instances, the need and expense of typed itineraries will have been eliminated by the use of duplicate hard copies.

There is, however, an even greater future ahead in other areas of automation. These include the time consuming tasks of fare construction and ticket writing. These are areas in which far greater cost savings can be realized if the systems are properly designed and economically used. In these areas we should look forward to great progress, but none will or can be accomplished overnight. All of these new features of automation are technically feasible today, but unfortunately the cost at the moment is prohibitive. Time should erase some of these problems and it is conceivable to expect some of these innovations by the latter part of this decade.

Another function in which automated equipment has a distinct future is in the area of information retrieval. It is possible to store all of the tariffs and information necessary to the operation of a travel agency on a reduced size microfilm called microfiche. The microfiche can be stored in such a way that specific pages of a tariff, hotel or destination information, health and visa requirements and schedules can be retrieved in seconds and displayed on a screen. This will eventually replace the many hours wasted in looking for information in out-of-date and hard-to-locate files. A system of this type will also eliminate the need for additional space for filing itself. It may even mean the end of much of the "junk" mail that floods the agency today.

I am confident that those agents who approach this decade of automation with open arms, but with inquiring minds, will gain a profitable ally.

Chapter 7

Communications Equipment

by

Roger M. Stillman

The term "communications" means different thing to different people. For the purpose of this material, it describes telephone, teletypewriter and facsimile equipment suitable for travel agencies.

Communications literature is incredibly hard to acquire. Often what is available tends to be too specialized or technical, and is scattered here and there in magazines or newspapers. The attempt here is to give the manager or owner of a travel agency enough information so that he can set up his office, or expand an existing office, with some thought given to the equipment he requires. In addition, this should be helpful information, too often lacking, in discussions with the local telephone company representative.

Each application and use of equipment will be based, of course, on local cost factors, equipment availability and office layout. This material is provided, therefore, as a basic guideline.

The Telephone System

Your telephone system must be able to receive calls, originate calls, transfer calls, intercept incoming calls if the called party is busy or unavailable, and provide internal communications. It should be adaptable for any size agency, from a minimum of two or three persons to a large agency of over 25.

Glossary of Telephone Terminology

"Telephone language" is not always understandable. Defined below are those terms most frequently used and common to all agencies.

Manual System — A switchboard with an operator attendant who answers all incoming calls and distributes them. Any person placing an outside call requests the operator to dial the number; the operator must disconnect after the call is completed. Interoffice communication is also placed through the operator.

Dial System — Performs many of the functions of the switchboard operator, who merely answers incoming calls and distributes them. Outgoing calls are placed by dialing a one- or two-digit number, receiving a dial tone from the local central office and dialing the number desired. Interoffice communication is connected by dialing a two- or three-digit extension number.

Central Office — The local exchange area. The central office for a Plaza 6-1234 number is PL6 (756). However, this is not true in large metropolitan areas, such as New York or Chicago, where there are many central offices in a given exchange area.

Exchange Area — A geographic area encompassing one or more central office locations. This is extremely important in areas where the telephone company offers various grades of service, such as flat rate and extended flat rate business service. (See "Telephone Number Billing Requirements.")

Local Call — A call within one, two or three given central office areas.

Toll Call — Any call outside your local calling area.

Local Service — The equipment either located in your premises, or tied in via a line, such as a tie line to another location. On your telephone bill, the "Equipment Charges" line, normally the first line, is the charge for local service.

142

Tie Line — A tie line is a direct electrical connection between two private branch exchange systems (PBX).

Private Branch (PBX) — Normally associated with a large subscriber. A PBX comprises a switching system and a console or switchboard on the subscriber's premises.

Key System — A push button telephone system with from two to thirty telephone lines. This enables the subscriber to pick up any given number of lines on a telephone.

Description of Equipment

Two line instruments provide the very small agency with a flexible arrangement whereby two lines may be answered on one or more telephone instruments. A turn-and-push button permits the telephone user to select either of the two lines. The pushbutton may also be used to activate a buzzer for signaling another telephone user.

Button Telephone Instruments

The telephone companies throughout the United States offer various types of telephone instruments. The buttons available range from that of a 3-line through 120-line instruments. Basically, all of the instruments perform the same functions; the only difference is the appearance and size.

Most instruments are available for both desk and wall mounting. The button instruments available are: 3, 6, 10, 12, 18, 20, 30, 40, 60, 80, 100, 120.

These instruments are used in conjunction with key telephone systems for direct access to various lines. These lines may be outside (central office telephone numbers), interoffice, switchboard or private lines. In addition, one button is utilized to place a call on hold on one or more lines.

Hands Free Telephones

The Hands Free Telephone is simply a loud speaker which amplifies the incoming voice and a microphone which transmits the outgoing voice, permitting a telephone conversation without use of the handset. The instrument is good for agencies which may require group discussions. It is exceptionally good for large group conferences, meetings, or for allowing a secretary to take notes on a call for future reference. *A note of caution:* Use of a Hands Free Telephone obviously means that the conversation is not private, as the incoming voice is amplified through the speaker. Also, this type of instrument is not practical where there is a great deal of background noise.

Headset Equipped Telephones

Most telephones can be arranged so that you may use an operator's headset in addition to the standard handset. You may wish to equip some of your personnel with operator's headsets so that they can have both hands free, enabling them to be more efficient in writing up sales orders, looking up OAG information for a client, etc. This type equipment is best suited for an agency which has a high volume of calls going into a given department. Check with your local telephone company to see what equipment best suits your needs.

Impaired Hearing and Weak Speech Telephones

Amplifier telephone sets amplify telephone conversation approximately 25 per cent for persons with either hearing or weak speech problems. Volume is adjusted by means of a variable control knob which is enclosed in the handset.

The equipment is not recommended for noisy locations, as noise is picked up by the transmitter and actually reproduced, making the outgoing signal stronger.

Intercommunications Systems ("Intercoms")

Manual

A manual intercommunications buzzer system is a line common to two or more telephone instruments within a given organization, especially useful in the small or medium-size travel agency. In a larger agency, this operation can be used very effectively between an executive and secretary.

One Path 9 Code Dial System

This dial intercom system utilizing your telephone equipment is available for a maximum of nine "codes," i.e., numbers. However, each

144

number, #8, for example, can be made to ring any number of phones keyed to the number "8."

This system is especially adaptable to small and medium-sized agencies, and is an extremely effective means of handling incoming calls by utilizing the intercom line to tell people at another instrument to "pick up." A *word of caution:* since the talking circuit is common and available to everyone, the system provides little privacy.

One Path 18 Code Dial System

An expanded version of the above permits twice as many numbers to be assigned. This system has the added advantage of privacy in that other phones are "locked out" of the conversation when the dialed phone is answered.

Two Path 36 Code Dial System

The same as above, but with a total capacity of 36 assigned numbers. Also, the two path system allows for two simultaneous private conversations.

Six Path 60 Code Dial System

Sixty numbers can be assigned with this very large system, and the six paths permit six simultaneous conversations. If your needs are this great, however, it may be well to investigate an independent intercom system in lieu of the phone connected systems which have been described.

Your telephone company representative will gladly give you advice.

Automatic Dialers

Automatic dialers may be extremely useful in those agencies which have a high volume of calls to frequently called numbers. Such devices are offered by the telephone companies on a monthly rental basis. Also, private vendors provide this equipment on an outright purchase arrangement.

One such simple device is the punched card type. The user prepunches a telephone number on a card, the card is then inserted into the telephone, a button is depressed and the machine automatically dials the telephone number. (The monthly rate is approximately $2.50 each.)

Another device is the magnetic tape dialer, which permits the recording of up to 1,000 telephone numbers in alphabetic order. These machines are very fast, but are only practical where the volume of outgoing calls clearly indicates such automation will be a substantial time and money saver. (The monthly rate is approximately $9.50 each.)

Manual Switchboards

Depending upon the size of your travel agency, a manual switchboard may fit your particular operation.

Switchboards range in size from a few trunks, or lines, to as many as you desire almost without limitation. The number of extensions which can be connected to the system is also virtually unlimited.

Although one must consider the added expense of employing a switchboard operator, the manual system can offer these advantages:

Daily record and thus better control of long distance charges.

Immediate direction of incoming calls to available personnel.

Assigns to the switchboard operator the task of placing and obtaining desired numbers, thus freeing the sales people for more productive work, expecially when the number called is busy or there are other delaying factors.

Use of the switchboard operator's free time for typing, filing and possibly other administrative duties.

Dial Systems

Telephone companies do offer their subscribers dial switchboard systems with some automatic features.

(1) *Dial Out Service (Dial "9")*

Dial out service permits outside dialing on extension telephones without going through your attendant, in which case consideration should be given to who should have the availability of dialing out.

146

Restricted telephones can still place calls to the outside by dialing "0" and requesting a line from the switchboard operator. The operator can be instructed to control these outside calls.

(2) *Interoffice Communications with Switchboard Dial Systems*
Interoffice communication with switchboard dial systems requires no effort on the part of your switchboard operator as outlined in manual systems. You simply dial the extension numbers as outlined in the "intercom" section above.

Series Dial Systems (Package Systems)

Series System # 200
Most telephone companies offer a Series (package) Communications Service, eliminating the need to sell a subscriber various individual pieces of hardware. This enables a prospective buyer to make a decision without trying to decipher various types of equipment and their functions.

Outlined below are those features which are normally offered in the Series System #200; however, because of complexity of the equipment, it is suggested that a representative review the Series with you.

(1) *Attendant Position.* The operator is normally provided with a desk-top console, the size of which depends entirely on the agency's needs. Operation of the console is relatively simple. The main duties of the operator are to receive incoming calls and direct them to the respective extensions, allowing her to assume other duties, such as typing, sorting and stuffing mail, etc., when call volume permits.

(2) *Direct Outward Dialing.* The extension user can dial outside without going through the switchboard attendant, by dialing "9," waiting for a dial tone, and then proceeding to dial the desired number.

(3) *Direct Inside Dialing.* An individual can automatically call another inside telephone without the operator's assistance by dialing the two- or three-digit code.

(4) *Station Hunting.* Incoming calls can be automatically routed to another extension number when a called extension is busy — a good feature when there is a common sharing of extension numbers. This feature also eliminates the need to redial another number when the first number dialed is busy.

(5) *Attendant Direct Station Selection.* The console operator has a lighted lamp panel that shows her which extension numbers are busy and which are free. If she desires to route an incoming call to an extension, she merely depresses the button associated with that extension number, automatically routing the call to that telephone.

(6) *Camp On.* This feature enables the attendant to hold a call on an extension line that is busy. The call will remain in the hold condition until the party completes his first conversation and hangs up his telephone, at which time the call on hold will automatically ring through.

(7) *Indication of Camp On.* When the operator places a call on *Camp On*, a soft tone will sound at the called station, indicating that another caller is waiting.

(8) *Call Transfer by Attendant.* An extension user may transfer an *incoming* call by depressing the switchhook plunger once. The automatic equipment will then continually signal the operator until she comes on the line.

(9) *Attendant Conference.* Conference calls with a number of persons are accomplished by dialing "0," giving the operator the telephone numbers and the persons to be called, internally and externally. She will set up the connections and call back when the call is ready.

(10) *Night Connections.* When the console is to be unattended (overnight, or for any reason), the operator selects the appropriate individual telephone extension numbers and connects outside telephone lines to them. An incoming call will thus ring on the extension to which it is connected.

148

(11) *Station Restriction.* You may restrict certain telephones so that they cannot be used for outside calls.

Series System # 300

The Series #300 is a more sophisticated system than the Series #200, offering additional features. In addition to the regular features on the Series #200, the Series #300 offers the following:

(1) *Consultation Hold (Incoming Calls Only).* In the case of telephones lacking buttons, incoming calls may be placed on hold by depressing the switchhook plunger once. An internal call may be made on the same instrument. Depressing the switchhook again returns the outside call. The outside caller cannot hear the intercom call while he is "on hold."

(2) *Add-on (Incoming Calls Only).* This permits an extension user to add another extension to an incoming call without operator assistance. A three-way conversation can be held by going through the *Consultation Hold* steps and depressing the switchhook once while the intercom party stays on the line.

(3) *Call Transfer – Individual (Incoming Calls Only).* Each extension user can transfer an incoming call to another extension without going through the console operator by going through the *Add On* procedures outlined above, then hanging up. The call will be automatically transferred, leaving the original extension called free for other calls.

(4) *Night Answering Service.* When the console is unattended, a special bell rings, after which any extension may pick up the call by dialing a preset code. These calls can then be transferred in the normal manner.

Typical Telephone Requirements

Check the section entitled "Telephone Number Billing Arrangements" to assure you have the most economical type of service available for your area. It may be good to remember, while reading this section, that when adding additional telephone *numbers,* you may reserve at no cost a consecutive number (or numbers) for future growth, provided that the number is not "working," i.e., in use for another telephone company subscriber.

Two-to Three-Person Offices

Requirements: Two incoming lines, consecutive numbers, which will provide two lines for incoming calls.

One outgoing line, separate from the incoming lines. This is one way costs can be watched; it is suggested that you insist that your people utilize this line when placing outgoing calls, at the same time freeing the two lines in the series group for incoming calls.

You may or may not need to have an intercom so that you can talk with each other, depending on office layout.

Equipment: Six-button telephones with the hold feature and lamps.

Call Operation: It may be best to have the telephone for one secretary ring on all calls so that she can answer for everyone.

Four-to Nine-Person Offices

Depending on the actual volume of telephone calls received in a particular office, we have tried to indicate which configuration constitutes the best telephone communication system.

Requirements: It may be that incoming traffic can be handled with three lines in a consecutive basis for incoming calls, as indicated in above for a 2-3 person office. In addition, persons who make many outgoing calls might have their own individual telephone numbers. It is extremely important to do research in this area. Various types of service are available so select the least expensive way to give proper, adequate service to all parties concerned. In no case should employees tie up the incoming lines for placing outgoing calls. If the telephone company only offers either flat rate or extended flat rate, you may desire to go into a twelve-button telephone, or you may wish to have six lines, or seven consecutive lines, used for incoming and outgoing

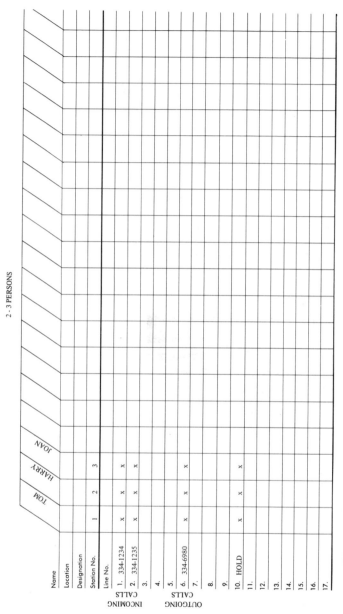

	TOM	HARRY	JOAN				
Name							
Location							
Designation							
Station No.	1	2	3				
Line No.							
INCOMING CALLS							
1. 334-1234	X	X	X				
2. 334-1235	X	X	X				
3.							
4.							
5.							
6. 334-6980	X	X	X				
OUTGOING CALLS							
7.							
8.							
9.							
10. HOLD	X	X					
11.							
12.							
13.							
14.							
15.							
16.							
17.							

All 6-button type telephone instruments.

All lines should have flashing lamps on incoming calls, steady lamps on answered or held calls. Optional: a winking light on held calls.

	Designation								
Name	EVA	JOAN	BETTY	MARION	TOM	DICK	HARRY	JOE	BILL
Location									
Designation									
Station No.									
Line No.	1	2	3	4	5	6	7	8	9
1. 334-1234	x	x	x	x	x	x	x	x	x
2. 334-1235	x	x	x	x	x	x	x	x	x
3. 334-1236	x	x	x	x	x	x	x	x	
4. 334-1237	x								
5. 334-1238		x							
6. 334-1239			x						
7. 334-1240				x					
8. 334-1241					x				
9.						x			
10.									
11. INTERCOM	x	x	x	x	x	x	x	x	x
12. HOLD	x	x	x	x	x	x	x	x	x
13.									
14.									
15.									
16.									
17.									

All 6-button type telephone instrument.

If a line appears on only one telephone, lights are not needed.

Incoming lines should have flashing lamps on incoming calls, steady lamp on answered calls and winking lights when a call has been answered and placed on hold.

152

4 - 9 PERSONS (ALTERNATE)

Name	EVA	JOAN	BETTY	MARION	TOM	DICK	HARRY	JOE	BILL
Location									
Designation									
Station No.	1	2	3	4	5	6	7	8	9
Line No.									
1. 334-1234	x	x	x	x	x	x	x	x	x
2. 334-1235	x	x	x	x	x	x	x	x	x
3. 334-1236	x	x	x	x	x	x	x	x	x
4. 334-1237	x	x	x	x	x	x	x	x	x
5. 334-1238	x	x	x	x	x	x	x	x	x
6. 334-1239	x	x	x	x	x	x	x	x	x
7. 334-1240	x	x	x	x	x	x	x	x	x
8. INTERCOM	x	x	x	x	x	x	x	x	x
9.									
10.									
11.									
12. HOLD	x	x	x	x	x	x	x	x	x
13.									
14.									
15.									
16.									
17.									

All twelve-button type telephone instruments.

153

ADMINISTRATIVE

Name		MARY	TOM	EVA	JOE	JOAN	HARRY	BILL	BETSY	PART TIMERS
Location		1Ω	1Ω	1Ω	1Ω	1Ω	2Ω	2Ω	2Ω	2Ω	1Ω	1Ω
Designation	A	B	C	D	E	F	G	H	I	J
Station No.	40	31	32	33	34	35	36	37	38	39
Line No.										
1. Pri 31	x	x	x							
2. Pri 32	x	x	x							
3. INTERCOM										
4.		S → Z	x	x						
5.		Z ← S								
6. Pri 33	x	x	x	x						
7. Pri 34	x	x	x	x	x					
8. INTERCOM				x	x					
9.				S → Z	x	x				
10.				Z ← S						
11. Pri 35						x	x	x		
12. Pri 36						x	x	x		
13. Pri 37						x	x	x		
14. Pri 38									LB	
15. Pri 39										LB
16. Pri 40	x									
17.										

Stations B–C–D–E–F–G–H are 6-button instruments.
Station A is a 12-button instrument.
Stations I–J are normal desk instruments.

S - Signal Button
Z - Buzzer
LB - One-line instrument

154

calls. In such cases, it is best not to assign individuals their own particular telephone numbers.

Equipment: Go to six-button telephones with three lines consecutive and assign each heavy user with his own outgoing line, or have twelve-button instruments throughout the entire organization with six or seven consecutive lines. It is suggested that some means of interoffice communication be provided so that incoming calls may pass from one party to another, thus eliminating the necessity of walking to talk. Check "Intercommunications Systems" section to select the most advantageous arrangement for your operation.

Seven-to Twenty-Person Offices

An agency with the number of employees in the teens is one most difficult for which to engineer a telephone system. The requirements are too large for a push button system and too small for a switchboard. A good deal of thought must therefore be given to office setup as well as telephone systems.

It is suggested that an agency of this size start out with a straight push button system where all persons can pick up all lines. However, as the agency grows, dividing the functions in terms of administrative, domestic sales and international sales should be considered.

After the system has reached the saturation point, and as employees are added, a complete review of the entire communication arrangement should be made to assure if the agency has reached the point where a switchboard-type system is required (see next section).

When an agency reaches twenty people, communications will break down if the proper telephone system is not employed. The flow of words and written communications is the backbone of any travel agency; therefore it is important that the system be carefully thought out in every conceivable fashion before implementation.

Here is a guide to assist in selecting the *best* system for your agency.

Administrative

As the agency grows, so should the telephone system. Perhaps it has now reached the size that some sort of switchboard or other system be employed to ease the flow of traffic.

It is suggested that the agency of twenty or more have a

switchboard, either manual or dial, depending on volume, to answer calls and distribute them to the appropriate persons.

A two-person unit arrangement should be employed where practical, with each having a button telephone which rings for the same extension number (i.e., Tom and Eva — #4). In addition, a manual intercom line permits one person to answer the calls, place the caller on hold, depress the intercom and announce the call to her co-worker.

The above setup can also be used very effectively for outside salesmen. However, other departments, such as accounting, may only require regular desk telephones, and in many instances two or three in a department can share the same telephone if the call volume is minimal.

Domestic Sales

Normally, sales personnel deal more with walk-in trade and may require a minimum of telephone coverage, again dependent on the particular agency.

It is suggested that two or three extension numbers on the number of instruments needed be a starting point, although additional lines may be required. Also, employment of direct outside lines may help if the calling volume is high.

International Sales

If an agency has a high volume of commercial clients, incoming calls can now be directed to this group without going through the main switchboard. There are many ways to provide adequate coverage in this department. For example:

(1)   Provide two lines from the switchboard for use on all international sales telephones for calls which come into the main switchboard.

(2)   Provide all sales and management personnel in the department with their own extension numbers for use in placing interoffice and outside calls. In addition, calls answered by the main switchboard for a specific person can be directed to him.

(3)   There should be a group (three or four) of direct outside telephone numbers which can be given to international accounts, eliminating the need for the caller to go through the main switchboard before reaching the sales person.

156

XYZ AGENCY

Line No.	Station No.	INTERNATIONAL SALES					DOMESTIC			ADMINISTRATIVE				MISC	MISC	
		A	B	C	D	E	F	G	H	I	J	K	L			
1.	334-1234	x	x	x	x	x	x	x	x	x	x	x	x	x	x	Listed as Sales &
2.	334-1235	x	x	x	x	x	x	x	x	x	x	x	x	x	x	Managerial
3.	334-1236	x	x	x	x	x	x	x	x	x	x	x	x	x	x	
4.	334-1237	x	x	x	x	x	x	x	x	x	x	x	x	x	x	
5.	334-9428	x	x	x	x	x										Listed as International
6.	334-9429	x	x	x	x	x										Sales
7.	334-9430	x	x	x	x	x										
8.	334-6429						x	x								Listed as Domestic
9.	334-6430						x	x								Sales
10.																
11.	HOLD	x	x	x	x	x	x	x	x	x	x	x	x	x	x	
12.	INTERCOM	x	x	x	x	x	x	x	x	x	x	x	x	x	x	
13.																
14.																
15.					The number of lines on a given telephone would determine the type instrument required.											
16.																
17.																

Alternative

(1) Provide a group of extension numbers from the switchboard, common to all international sales persons' telephones, giving complete coverage on any of the lines.

(2) Again, a direct outside number group should appear on all of the instruments.

(3) Some management personnel may require individual extensions of their own which do not appear on the sales phones.

In any case, one person should be assigned "backup" duty with the availability to all of the lines on his telephone. If someone is away from his desk, the line is still "covered."

Services Available

Private Line — For a large travel agency, a private line may be installed as a direct line from the agency office to a client office. This service offers many advantages: there are no delays or interruptions to communications with the client; you know exactly who is calling, the

frequency of his calls and the kind of requests he normally makes, and can gear your operation for priority service to this client; there may be savings over normal service charges for toll and message unit costs, and the client may be willing to assume a percentage or all of the private line charges.

Foreign Exchange Lines — A foreign exchange line actually brings a telephone number from a distant area or city into an agency. It offers toll free calling to you and your clients in that area with only a possible message unit charge. Many times this reduces long distance charges, which more than offsets the total cost of the service.

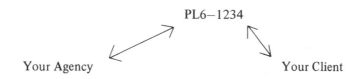

PITTSBURGH   *PHILADELPHIA*

PL6–1234

Your Agency   Your Client

Hotline — Hotline service is offered only by Western Union and is a point-to-point voice communication service on a measured rate basis. Specific locations have a hotline telephone with no dial or buttons. Picking up the handset triggers an automatic ring at the other location. The service is presently available only between several major cities in the United States, but Western Union is adding additional cities. Those agencies which subscribe to this service are furnished with a main station telephone and with additional extension phones, as required.

Hotline service is billed in increments of six seconds and only for the actual time used on the line. *No 10 per cent* federal tax applies. There is a monthly charge, in addition, for the main station and for each extension, as well as an installation charge for each service station. Rates vary for service from city to city.

This service would only be beneficial to an agency with multi-locations where direct communication is high, and expedience is important.

NEW YORK   *LOS ANGELES*

Your Agency   ⟵―――――――⟶   Your
                                                              Branch Agency

Wide Area Telephone Service (WATS) — WATS is ideal for the travel agent who does a large amount of calling to widely scattered and distant points. All calls must be dialed direct and not placed through an operator. The agency pays a monthly rate for each line designated as a WATS line. Service is available for Full Time and Measured Time.

> *Full Time* — gives unlimited calling in the WATS area you select.
> *Measured Time* — gives a minimum of ten hours of actual talking time per month in the WATS area selected. Time is measured from the moment the called party's line is answered. Any time in excess of ten hours is charged on a per hour basis. A WATS line may be established with all types of telephone equipment, including switchboards and call directors.
> *Zones* — There are six WATS areas. An agent may subscribe to Zone 1, which includes those areas basically contiguous to his own home state, or to any or all of the five other Zones. Your local telephone company can provide a WATS breakdown for both monthly cost and the geographic areas which each Zone comprises.
> *Limitations* — WATS lines can not be used for person-to-person, credit card or collect calls, nor can you have the Operator place calls. All calls must be dialed direct. Conference calls only within the office at either end of the WATS line can be arranged.

Inward WATS — If you so desire you can encourage your clients to call you on a "collect call" basis through use of an Inward WATS line number on which calls are charged to you on a flat monthly fee or measured rate basis (see above). This type of service encourages clients to call you in preference to your competitors, and is particularly suited to larger agencies where volume substantiates the cost.

Outward WATS — You can subscribe to selected geographic areas throughout the United States, outside of your home state, for use in calling respective clients, airlines, steamship companies, etc., without incurring large conventional toll charges. Again, this line may be subscribed to on either a full or measured time basis as described in the Inward WATS section. It is well to inform your employees that this line is to be used as infrequently as possible if you are subscribing on a measured rate basis so as to avoid excessive overtime rates. Too often, there is a misunderstanding of the use of WATS lines in the sense that calls are not free; you pay for use of these lines and your telephone company representative or a private consulting firm should assist you in learning how to use them wisely.

Intrastate WATS — You may subscribe to the WATS within your home state, available for both Inward and Outward Service. In larger states you may find that you can subscribe to a portion of the state.

Special Reversed Charge Toll Service — Charges for long distance calls can be automatically reversed to the called agency without the specific request of the calling client. This service is offered on a selected basis to one or more exchange areas as desired. A caller in the subscribed-to area, outside the agency's local calling area and usually where there is a concentration of clients, dials the Operator and gives her the special Enterprise, Zenith or WX number. The operator completes the connection and charges the agency for the call. This is a fairly inexpensive way to offer clients a way to communicate with you free of charge. It avoids business lost because of trouble, inconvenience and possible refused collect calls.

You may desire to give the special reverse charge number only to specific clients. This would avoid many calls which would be unproductive.

Telephone Answering Services

Secretarial Services

Almost everywhere there are answering services for use when your office is unattended or when you do not wish to be disturbed. This is an especially useful service for smaller offices.

Listed in the Yellow Pages of your local directory, under "Telephone Answering Services," are companies which can meet these needs:

1. Answering unattended telephones 24 hours a day.
2. Answering after the agency has closed for the day or on weekends, if this is your need, or
3. Answering the telephone if you do not want to be disturbed for a period of time (if, for example, you are the only person in the office trying to close an important sale free of interruption).

This service will take messages and relay them to the agency each day, or whenever requested. If an emergency arises, the service can be instructed to call someone in authority to obtain immediate action.

The monthly cost of these services can range from $12 up, depending upon your volume and the type of service you require.

Automatic Answering Devices

Equipment which actually answers the telephone can be rented or purchased. This equipment can be arranged so that it gives pre-recorded information to the caller and receives incoming messages. Messages can be retrieved at any time by the agency personnel.

The equipment is offered on a monthly rental basis by your local telephone company and can be purchased, rented, or lease-purchased from private suppliers, of which there are many.

If you elect to use a private supplier, the telephone company *must* provide an interconnection device to protect the equipment. The rates vary from $2 and up per month.

A direct electrical connection of private equipment to telephone company equipment is *not permitted*. Check with the local telephone company before installing private equipment to assure that the connection is proper.

Your Telephone Costs

Telephone Number Billing Arrangements

Telephone companies offer various billing arrangements according to the grades of service subscribed to. To see what service the telephone company in your particular area offers, check in the front of the local telephone directory, or have the telephone company explain the various grades of service.

162

Itemized here are grades of service normally offered in most parts of the United States.

Message Rate Service — Within a *very limited* calling area you are charged a flat rate per call, regardless of the length of the call. Once the local calling area is exceeded, the telephone company will bill on a multi-message unit basis; that is, a two or three message unit minimum, with additional message units being charged for additional minutes of use.

Flat Rate Service — With this service, as many calls as desired may be made within a small geographic area for a fixed monthly cost for each line.

Inward Only Service — Certain telephone numbers may be restricted to receive only incoming calls. Often the telephone company will offer a reduced rate for this service, because it doesn't have to tie up equipment to provide outgoing dial tones. If your company has a large volume of incoming calls, it may be worthwhile to see if this service is offered in your locale. This service may only be practical when terminating telephone numbers on a switchboard with a Key System arrangement. Where numbers terminate on push button telephones, this service normally is not available.

Cost Control Sheets

Many times, agents take telephone costs for granted and pay invoices without even cursory checking. In order to get a true picture of your total costs for communications, it may be well to incorporate the forms "Monthly Billing Itemization" and "Total Billing Log" in your monthly accounting procedures.

Monthly Billing Itemization — Each month a telephone bill is received for advance service and all of the charges for the previous month. Items on the bill should be filled in on the Monthly Billing Itemization Form as follows:

1. *Service and Equipment* — This charge, billed one month in advance, covers all of the telephone equipment and lines which you have. This figure should change *only* when you request a change be made to add or reduce equipment, or when there is a rate increase or decrease.

163

MONTHLY BILLING ITEMIZATION

MONTH	S & E	M. U.	M.U. $	IC	DIR ADV	OCC	TAX			BAL	TOTAL
JANUARY											
FEBRUARY											
MARCH											
APRIL											
MAY											
JUNE	(1)	(2)	(3)	(4)	(5)	(6)	(7)	(8)	(9)	(10)	(11)
JULY											
AUGUST											
SEPTEMBER											
OCTOBER											
NOVEMBER											
DECEMBER											
TOTALS											

YEAR _____

TELEPHONE BILLING NUMBER _____ (12)

164

TOTAL BILLING LOG

BILLING NUMBER	JAN	FEB	MAR	APR	MAY	JUN	JULY	AUG	SEPT	OCT	NOV	DEC	YEAR TOTAL
(1)	(2)	(2)	(2)	(2)	(2)	(2)	(2)	(2)	(2)	(2)	(2)	(2)	(4)
MONTHLY TOTAL	(3)												

(1) Enter billing number
(2) Enter total amount of telephone bill, minus any balance
     from last bill
(3) Totals for the month
(4) Totals for the year, for each billing number

165

2. *Message Units* – This figure represents the number of message unit calls you have been charged.
3. *Message Unit Charges* – This is the cost for local message unit calls.
4. *Itemized Charges – Long Distance Calls* – A complete review should be made each month to verify that each call listed was actually placed.
5. *Directory Advertising* – This represents the monthly cost of Yellow Page directory advertising.
6. *Other Charges and Credits* – A pro-rata charge made each time a change is made in equipment. If a piece of equipment is removed, a credit will be given for service paid in advance for the unused balance of the billing period. If, on the other hand, a piece of equipment is added, a debit will be noted for the balance of the billing period. Listed here will be service connection charges, installation charges, specialty entries, such as credits or debits for equipment which has or has not been billed, message units, charges for certain foreign exchange lines and other miscellaneous charges or credits.
7. *Taxes* – Applicable taxes, state and local, and 10 per cent federal tax on all calls.
8- Columns are available for other entries pertinent to your particular
9. telephone bill and your operation.
10. *Balance from Last Bill* – Any amount owed from previous bills appears here.
11. *Total Amount Due* – Total of this month's charges.
12. *Telephone Number* – (Form should be completed for each telephone number for which you receive a bill.) Enter the telephone number billed here.

Now enter each month's telephone service costs in the "Total Billing Log." Inasmuch as travel is seasonal, you can now project costs for telephone service in direct relationship to gross business. You may desire to make adjustments in your service during slow periods of the year.

Directory Listings

A thorough review of all your agency listings in the various directories in your market area should be made. It is suggested that you

166

do not use BOLD TYPE in the white alphabetical listings, since anyone looking up your firm is looking for your specific name, and the bold type is an unnecessary added expense.

Equipment Inventory and Review

The first line on a telephone bill normally represents the monthly rental charge for all telephone equipment and lines which are utilized. It behooves the agent to review these charges periodically.

Call the local telephone company business office and request a breakdown of all equipment charges. Upon receiving the breakdown, review the list and take a physical inventory of *all* equipment. If you do not thoroughly understand some explanation or cannot find some of the equipment, request that a telephone company representative visit your office.

If discrepancies are found, bring it to the attention of the telephone company business office. If they been overbilling, request a refund back to the date when the error occurred. In addition, you are entitled to a refund on the tax which applies to that particular item charge. Many telephone companies will also provide a subscriber with interest on amounts which will be refunded.

Periodic reviews should be made to ascertain that the communications equipment, once selected as the most suitable for your operation, is still performing as designed. Can some of the services be reduced or eliminated to obtain savings while maintaining the required performance? If service is now inadequate, will a change in office procedures be sufficient to restore service to the proper level? Will any changes be valid six months or one year later? Excess equipment increases your operating costs and reduces profits; insufficient equipment endangers your communications and inhibits earnings and profits.

Toll Analysis

The telephone bill received monthly from the telephone company itemizes all of the long distance calls which your firm had made for the preceding month. It may be profitable to analyze those calls to see if some sort of WATS application might economically apply to your particular operation.

The following page shows a toll analysis work sheet for use in breaking down your calls by number and cost. To obtain a call breakdown by minutes, ask the telephone company for the total lapsed time for each individual call. After breaking down your calls by given area, contact the telephone company again and ask them to review your findings for possible WATS application.

Other Communications Equipment

FACSIMILE TRANSMISSION SYSTEMS

Facsimile telephone equipment provides instantaneous, error-free transmission of copies of documents to remote locations in as little as a minute. A copy or original of the document to be transmitted is placed in the equipment and the user dials the telephone number of the destination to which the facsimile document is to go. After communication between the two telephones has been established, the machine is placed in a "send" mode and the information transmitted.

Some companies offer unattended service wherein the equipment answers and receives the document without an operator. After the call has been completed the machine automatically shuts off.

At this particular time it may be that there is limited application for travel agencies, small or large. However, this is a coming thing, after unit costs decline somewhat and the equipment is simplified.

If you are interested, check with a local supplier of facsimile equipment who will provide prices, suggested applications and procedures.

TWX (TELETYPEWRITER EXCHANGE SERVICE)

TWX Service provides two-way written communication between two or more subscribers. Each subscriber has a sending and receiving typewriter (either manual or automatic, depending upon individual customer requirements). A subscriber dials the number of a distant TWX subscriber, as with telephone service.

TOLL ANALYSIS WORKSHEET

AREA CODE MONTH	TOTAL NUMBER CALLS	TOTAL COST	TOTAL MINUTES	TOTAL NUMBER CALLS	TOTAL COST	TOTAL MINUTES	TOTAL NUMBER CALLS	TOTAL COST	TOTAL MINUTES
JANUARY									
FEBRUARY									
MARCH									
APRIL									
MAY									
JUNE									
JULY									
AUGUST									
SEPTEMBER									
OCTOBER									
NOVEMBER									
DECEMBER									
TOTALS									

169

Charges are applied as follows:

In Continental U.S.A. — Local area (intra-exchange). One-minute minimum per connection, plus additional time charges.

Interstate Calls — One-minute minimum per connection, with additional minutes charged at the same rate.

In Canada — Same as Interstate Calls.

Information is transmitted at a rate up to 60 to 100 words per minute. All Canadian TWX subscribers have 100 WPM speed service.

Operator assistance (954-1212) is available when calls are not dialed directly, or for time-charge information, TWX conference calls, TWX collect calls, and TWX overseas calls. TWX information is 910-555-1212.

A TWX Directory provides the following information:
All continental U.S.A. and Canadian subscribers.
White pages list alphabetically by state and city.
Yellow pages list by business classification.
Individual customer identification (answer back).

Several models are available depending upon required speed and features. Your telephone company representative is responsible for the ordering of the equipment and the training of personnel.

Chapter 8

Travel Agency Marketing

by

Walter J. Mathews

Marketing/Evolution

Travel in the U.S. today is big. So big that we can be misled if we fail to keep it in perspective.

In 1969, Americans spent $29.7 billion on domestic travel for all purposes, compared to $5.4 billion on foreign travel, most of which was to Canada, with $1.8 billion being spent for overseas travel.

Air travel has been growing at a rate of 16 to 20 per cent a year. It is also a fact that 80 per cent of pleasure trips in the U.S. are still taken by automobiles — that some 56 million families do have the time, the money, and do travel on vacations of more than 200 miles, but don't go near an airline or a travel agent.

Although there are some moves to package auto tours, it is recognized that the agent is tied almost directly to the airlines. The airline industry controls entry into the agency business. The majority of travel agency commissions come from ticketing air travel arrangements. And the carriers are just about as dependent on the agents. For example, the 6000-plus travel agents in the U.S. provide from 40 to 90 per cent of the airlines' revenues, with domestic carriers being on the low side, and the smaller foreign carriers in the 90 per cent bracket.

Until the advent of the airplane for commercial use after World War II, the people who traveled were, for the most part, businessmen or "seasoned" and experienced pleasure travelers. Because of their education, upbringing, and income, they considered travel, i.e., the *needs* for the kinds of products sold by the travel agent, a necessary part of their way of life. Travel, other than automobile, was by ship or rail. A "March of Time" film, reporting on the "booming" travel business in 1946, made only one reference to air travel.

Most of the arrangements made by the travel agent were individual. During this same time, the automobile and gasoline companies were promoting the idea of traveling by automobile, with services such as maps, tour planning assistance and rest rooms.

Following World War II, the airlines, through great risk-taking by highly individualistic and courageous leaders, began to provide safe, efficient, dependable air transportation. As the product improved, the businessman saw it as a way to expand his markets. As he did, so did his competition.

Even now, approximately 60 per cent of domestic U.S. air travel and 20 per cent of overseas air travel is for business purposes. Most of the airlines felt they could best sell this business directly, with the result that the travel agent's role became that of selling foreign vacation travel. His customers were, though greater in number, still the more affluent, educated. The median income and age of the trans-Atlantic air traveler have not changed significantly since 1964. While more lower income people are traveling, so are the more higher income people. The same is true of age. The most recent Port of New York Authority Study of the Trans-Atlantic traveler (1968) shows his median age to be 43 and his income to be $14,500.

Years ago, this market was relatively easy to identify and to understand. The existing machinery (advertising, travel agent) worked reasonably well to attract this market, being fairly homogeneous in character.

Now, the question is how to continue to grow, profitably — how to get more people to travel, and make money doing so.

All of this points up a growing recognition on the part of most segments of the travel industry for the need for marketing know-how, for a travel industry working together.

What is Marketing? And Why?

In this travel industry, marketing as a recognized function is a very new development. Although the term "marketing" has become popular in recent years and the title "Marketing Executive" became a part of some organizations in the early 1960's, to a great degree, it still is understood to mean "marketing a product," to mean "we have the product, let's find the customer and sell him." Marketing is too often thought of as just selling.

We hope to show that this is not the case — that marketing is a philosophy and a concept; it is an action and a collection of activities.

It is a philosophy in that it is based on the recognition that in a democratic and free enterprise system, the ultimate power over an organization or corporation rests with the customers/consumers. It is a business concept that suggests looking at one's products and services from the outside, from the customer's viewpoint, rather than from the inside. It is customer-oriented, as opposed to product- or supplier-oriented. What does the customer want? What does the customer think is the right price, or what is he willing to pay? How does the customer want to be told what is available? At what location, or through what "distribution channel," would the customer like to receive what's available?

Marketing is action, too. Here's where it is most often thought of as sales. As business people we instinctively realize no "business" really takes place (no opportunity for revenue and profits) until a sale takes place. The sale, the big action, is the transfer of cash (or other appropriate payment) from the customer to you for your product and service.

Other actions that best prepare you to consummate the sale *and to repeat sales* are the parts or activities of marketing we will soon examine in depth.

For our purposes, let's select just one of many ways marketing can be defined: it's the practice of best serving current customers and developing new customers by objectively trying to understand people, what they value, what they want, and then, designing, producing and selling products specifically for those people — and making money doing so.

The man who uses marketing views his business through the eyes of his customer or potential customers first. The non-marketing man, however, looks first at the products he has and then tries to find customers for them.

Marketing came about because of the need to more efficiently identify and sell to customers. Because it has been made to seem complicated, the small businessman tends to fear or think that marketing is not for him. This is nonsense. Many good small businessmen, including travel agents, are excellent marketing men. They practice it every day, but don't call it "marketing." Even with all the new language, computers and tools, the essential ingredient in marketing is still *judgment*. It can be useful to you, the travel agent, if you understand this concept.

It is understandable that the "state of the art" of marketing in the travel business is not, at this point, highly developed. We predict that it will advance rapidly, however, and trust this "do-able" approach will help.

Things are more easily understood (and remembered) when segmented and studied in their parts. Remember, our objective is increased profitable sales. All right, then.

Marketing consists of three basic parts:

1. *Research.* Who is the customer? What is he like? What will he buy?

2. *Product Design.* What kind of product(s) can best attract this customer? What should the product consist of? What should the price be? What are the real benefits, from the clients's viewpoint?

3. *Merchandising,* or *Action in the Marketplace.* How can the product and its benefits be most efficiently sold to the customer?

Also remember that marketing is not a process with a beginning and an end. Rather, it is a cycle constantly repeating itself, adjusting to changing conditions, acting on new opportunities.

To insure the application of marketing, periodically in the cycle there must be a plan, set down in writing. However simple, the plan must answer these questions:

Where are we going?

How are we going to get there?

How are we going to remain flexible?

How are we going to make money?

174

Without the plan, thoughtful intentions are too frequently forgotten and results unrelated. You can't decide how to do it differently on the next go 'round.

Research

People *do* differ. In this business of travel, it is the job of research to find out how they differ, and then to group those together who might be motivated by a particular set of appeals, and to determine the language and best means to reach them.

Unless we thoroughly understand what it is that an individual or group values, we may be trying to sell the wrong things, make the wrong appeals and lose the sales. Worse, perhaps we may underprice the product and make a lot of sales, with no profit.

It is the identification of values — what people want, what they like or dislike, their viewpoints, how they associate or refuse to associate with a given idea or product, their deeply-held beliefs — which permits us to design products and price them profitably.

What does all this mean to you, the travel agent? It means that your major suppliers in the travel business, such as the airlines, steamship companies and larger operators, as well as advertising media, are beginning to study market segments or groups in terms of customer interests, likes and dislikes, and their motivations, much more helpful information than just occupation, age, sex, income or other numbers, and to design programs for these market segments. When you are aware of this and knowledgeable, you will be able to improve the efficiency of your promotional effort. You can then tailor and conduct your promotional and sales approach toward those market groups which you are best able to serve.

To do this, you need to decide what persons and organizations (customer targets) you're going after. What is your market? If you don't know, begin by asking basic questions about the available potential of customers. Who lives in your particular area? Who can be served: an entire city, a suburb, a business area, parts of several different geographical areas, or particular groups (ethnic, student, military, etc.) without a particular geographical boundary? What organizations exist? You must be flexible and open to all possibilities. Start fresh, with no preconceived notions that a particular area holds no

175

potential for you because you've had no business from there in the past. Or that you've tried something before and it didn't work then.

How do you, a travel agent working long hours to keep the doors open, go about examining this?

It isn't that difficult.

The best way is to start with a map, preferably one with zip code boundaries shown. We mentioned earlier it might be an entire state, suburb, or city.

The task now is to learn as much as possible about your area, the people and businesses who are there, so that later you can select those persons and organizations which represent the best potential to you.

There are many sources. One is the U.S. Census Tract. Some of the 1970 Census data will be broken down by zip code. Zip codes are particularly useful boundaries. Because they are designed to facilitate the movement of mail, they tend to reflect the flow of business in a particular locality. They provide helpful clues to the economic and social make-up of the areas they represent. Such data as number of households, occupation, age and income is available.

Another source is local newspapers. If you are in or near a city of any size, your newspaper will have probably done some research of your market and its buying power for the purposes of selling advertising. In larger cities, some studies may deal specifically with travel. Others may be more general.

Your Chamber of Commerce can be a good source for lists of organizations, associations and other population and business data. The location of corporate branch offices can give you clues to travel patterns to company headquarters, or vice-versa. The Chamber's membership lists can give you a good lead on companies which may have business travel.

Your bank is another good source. It's in the bank's interest that you be successful, and they usually know the community well.

Religious organizations are often useful resources. Sometimes they themselves have travel potential.

Listed below are some research studies available to the public which may be helpful to you in identifying your potential customers and in putting together the right products. Check your local library, or write

176

the individual at the address indicated. The *source* of the publication or study is listed first in *italics*.

Travel Research Studies and Information Sources of Interest

American Society of Travel Agents, ASTA Research Project, 360 Lexington Avenue, New York, New York 10017

Better Homes and Gardens, "A Report on Family Travel" Ted Standish, Better Homes and Gardens Travel Marketing Manager, 750 Third Avenue, New York, New York 10017

Holiday Magazine, "The Creative Consumer" Holiday Magazine, 641 Lexington Avenue, New York, New York 10022

Negro Travel & Conventioneer Magazine, "Economic Impact of the Negro Traveler" Clarence M. Markham, Jr., Editor, Travelers Research Publishing Company, 8034 South Prairie Avenue, Chicago, Illinois 60619

Newsweek Magazine, "The Sindlinger Study" Richard Ludlow, Newsweek Magazine, 444 Madison Avenue, New York, New York 10017

PATA, "The Pacific Area: Charting Future Courses" PATA Research Department, 228 Grant Avenue, San Francisco, California 94108

ASTA Travel News, "The Big Picture" William D. Patterson, author, 488 Madison Avenue, New York, New York 10022

Port of New York Authority, "Domestic Air Passenger Market" Chief, Aviation Economics Division, Aviation Department, The Port of New York Authority, 111 Eighth Avenue, New York, New York 10011

Sports Illustrated, "A Study of the Role of Husband and Wife in Air Travel Decisions" William K. Ely, Market Research Manager, Sports Illustrated, Time and Life Building, New York, New York 10020

Time Magazine, "Off-Season Travel" Time Magazine, Time and Life Building, New York, New York 10020

Travel Market Yearbook, Marketing Handbooks, Inc., 820 Second Avenue New York, New York 10017

Bureau of Census, U.S. Department of Commerce, U.S. Census of Transportation, Superintendent of Documents, Washington, D.C. 20233

Travel Research International, "Vacation Attitude Study" Robert
Peattie 405 Lexington Avenue, New York, New York 10017

National Geographic, "A Study of Life-Style" William Wells and
others, authors, published by University of Chicago and Leo
Burnett, Peter Michaels, National Geographic, 630 Fifth Avenue,
New York, New York 10020

Reader's Digest (the following articles are based on motivational
research studies) "Should You Travel More?" "Questions People
Ask About Flying" "Should the Airlines Write You Off as
Hopeless?" George Wallace, Reader's Digest, Pan Am Building, New
York, New York 10017

In addition, the Travel Research Association periodically publishes
in their newsletter lists of new research studies.

In larger communities, some of the principals, particularly airlines,
are beginning to conduct market analyses. Ask your sales representatives or district managers if any of them have done so.

Internal research can also be helpful. Examination of your customer
records can tell you what kinds of people and organizations you have
served successfully in the past. There may be clues here... seek out
other, similar groups. Just the customer addresses alone can be helpful
to you in determining target geographic boundaries, or, that in fact
there is *no* pattern and probably will not be one in the future.

Examination of previous sales records, of course, also gives you an
indication as to which have been the most profitable customers and
most profitable products you have sold (taking into account the time
and related costs to sell those customers and products). There is no
sense in selecting a target market if this segment or the type of products
likely to be purchased by this segment do not produce profitable
business.

There are other sources, but this should give you the idea. You
shouldn't be satisfied until you've completely explored the paths we
suggested earlier.

From all of this, and with competition taken into consideration,
decide what's best for you and which segments you're going to go after.
Yes, it will take some time.

Product ✈

Every business has some products which are more profitable than others. But this is not to say that some customers don't find some products essential, or more valuable, than others, regardless of whether the most valuable product in the customer's eye is the most profitable product to the seller.

The importance of understanding customer needs or values has been discussed. Whether a group or an individual, once the needs and values have been established, the next task is to design or select the right products for the customer or group, building in as many of his values as possible.

Normally by "travel product" the following would be included:

Transportation tickets
Sightseeing services
Car hire, both domestic and foreign
Foreign car purchase
General travel consultation
Specific itinerary planning

Information on all types of accommodations

Delivery of tickets

Quotation of fare, rates, and other prices

Foreign currency and exchange facilities

Obtaining passports, visas and sailing permits

Arranging transfers between docks, airports and hotels

Reservations and arrangements for special interest groups, e.g., religious pilgrimages, conventions, hunting and other sporting trips, etc.

Travel and baggage insurance

Climate information

Health regulation information

Advice on language study and guidebook material

Shopping suggestions.

But there are other ways to look at the travel product too. As the only retailer where all of the travel components can be brought together, you benefit from knowing all of the ways your customers might look at what you have to offer.

What do we mean by "travel product?" One way to look at it is on a chronological basis, as travel occurs to the customer:

1. Planning
2. Anticipation
3. Getting there
4. Doing it
5. Getting back
6. Remembrance

All of the elements are important, but the planning and anticipation, as well as the remembrance, are seldom given the attention they deserve. Yet these are the areas where you, as an agent, can be most innovative and exert the greatest control.

Another useful way to look at or define the travel product is to divide it into its more tangible parts.

Every travel product contains these elements:

1. *Destination(s).* (Even the "cruise to nowhere.")
2. *Time factor.* Schedules, length of stay, itinerary.
3. *Accommodations, transportation.* Hotels, air, ship.

4. *Services.* Both enroute and at destination.

5. *Price.* (Only in relation to the above four elements.)

Each different combination of the above constitutes a different product. For example, the destination, time factor and services can remain the same, but an ocean-front hotel *room* is different from an ocean-front hotel. An overnight flight is a different product from a day flight, even though the tour may be the same. Fitting all of these together in just the right combination to give your client maximum value, and you maximum income, is not easy. But it's worth the effort.

Looking at these elements of the overall travel product, it becomes clear that you can "manufacture" literally countless different individual products. Then, to one destination alone, such as Hawaii, you have more products available than has the average supermarket — 5,000.

As every good salesman knows, thorough *product knowledge* is very important. With so many different products and constantly changing situations (politics, facilities, economics) around the world, keeping up to date is one of the agent's greatest challenges. He must know about all transportation to and within all countries of the world. This includes car rentals, buses, taxis, ferry schedules, walla walla transfers in Hong Kong, rail, ship, bicycle rental and even the cost of a donkey, elephant or camel rental in Egypt.

One of the developments in the past few years has been the introduction of familiarization trips. A well-organized, hard-working familiarization trip is obviously the best possible way to become familiar with travel products — in other words, to try it yourself.

It is just as obvious that it is impossible to visit often enough all the destinations you are called upon to sell. Regrettably, not yet is there a data bank and information retrieval system travel agents and others can call upon for the myriad kinds of knowledge customers seek or agents should provide. In addition to the personal knowledge you attain and carry in your head, the agency "library" and various reference files, there are, however, other ways of acquiring and up-dating your product knowledge.

As a specialist, the wholesaler is constantly in touch with destination hotels and operators. He may be able to answer your questions regarding his tour products and destinations.

Another good source of product knowledge is the trade press. While usually not so critical as they might be, the various trade publications do report regularly on new developments at destinations throughout the world.

Seminars are another means of up-dating product knowledge. These have been improving over the years as the sponsors begin to realize that most agents are serious business people who are anxious to learn, rather than people who are out simply for a free drink.

Some sales representatives can also be a good source of destination knowledge as well as their own products (hotel, airline, car rental). Get to know those who are and make good use of them.

There are other sources, too. If you are in or near a large city, there may be government tourist offices where staff can be helpful. They also have materials to help you answer your clients' questions or to heighten his anticipation of the trip.

Saving the best for last, there is no better source of product knowledge than returning clients. This is something many agents overlook.

Merchandising, or "Action in the Marketplace"

Everything we've talked about so far was only preparation for this discussion of merchandising, or what we prefer to call Action. Nothing happens unless you do something in the marketplace to communicate and sell to the specific customer or groups discussed earlier.

You can know a customer intimately, you can put together exactly the right product for him, but unless he knows it and buys it, and unless the whole exercise was profitable to you, what's the point? That's also why we put the word "Action" in the sub-title here.

Let's begin with a few admonitions:
1. Your most valuable commodity is time.
2. There must be a plan, however simple.
3. Don't try to go it alone. By coordinating with others, 2 plus 2 can make 5.

We'll start with the first. How you spend your time and the time of your people will have most to do with your degree of success

If you have your business/marketing plan and your organization of assistants and teammates, including the cooperating suppliers (admonitions 2 and 3, and the rest of this book!) then you can maximize your selling. You must be organized, rested and knowledgeable — but question every minute not applied to selling or developing prospects. These minutes may represent costly lost opportunity.

Second, there's the plan. We mentioned earlier that marketing is a logical, knowledgeable, organized approach to business, provided it is planned. What is a plan? It is deciding in the present what to do in the future. It's a process whereby you look at your strengths and opportunities, make objectives, and reconcile these objectives with your resources and the competitive environment. The plan does not become the stern taskmaster of your agency, but it should be the guideline by which you operate your business over a given period of time. Without it, your business runs you.

The first time you reduce a plan to writing is the most difficult. Each subsequent year, or other time period you might use for measurement, it will become easier.

The plan might contain some challenging yet attainable goals — for example, increasing gross sales per employee to $210,000 per year, and upping the agency average commission to 7 per cent.

This brings up the third point — don't try to go it alone. One reason is economic. With today's commission structure, you probably can't afford it. The other is that you'll make much greater impact if you coordinate your efforts with those of your suppliers and principals. But coordination requires that plan, or it can't work.

To get started, we suggest you write or call the various sales reps or suppliers. Ask them what their advertising plans are. What will the campaign feature? When will it take place? Do they have any special promotions coming up? If so, when can you have a chance to see if you can or want to tie in? What new materials will be available (displays, mailing pieces, brochures, etc.). What might you do together?

Obviously, you can't cover all the people with whom you do business. But you can cover those most important to you. Don't wait for them to come to you. Call or write to them. Those that respond will appreciate your wanting to work with them, particularly if you are calling to see how you both can get more business, rather than a tour or seat in the high season.

As you accomplish this, arrange the activities by month or quarter, and summarize a description of each so you can later see how it fits in with the notes you made earlier about the people you want to sell and the products they are most likely to buy.

To review, we have discussed researching your market and making up an inventory of the kinds of products that are most likely salable, and when.

That was followed by the suggestion that you find out what's going to be available from your suppliers in the way of both products and merchandising aids.

The next step is to look at yourself. What are your agency's resources? We're going to discuss some of them briefly. Our purpose is to show the kinds of actions that might be considered under merchandising. To do it justice, each category should have several chapters of its own. We expect only to take each one to the point where you can see how it may contribute to your overall results.

Direct Sales

By this we mean not only your ability to sell to those people who come in to your agency, but going out to prospects as well.

Direct sales solicited outside the agency can usually be justified only for volume accounts, such as incentives or other groups. It's sometimes possible to get a salesman on a one-shot deal, such as a special-interest tour or school group. Another possibility is to make greater use of the sales rep who calls on you. If he, or you, has a group in mind, suggest you try jointly to make the sale. The two of you will have greater impact and present a more persuasive image to the prospect.

However you decide to go about direct, or outside, sales, be sure you examine the dollar figures: cost plus your usual overhead for operations must be added and still show a profit for you.

Whether it's inside or outside, let's talk about the selling part for a few moments. *Selling is different from order taking.* Selling can turn a 5 per cent order into a 10 per cent sale. It's your job, and you want a satisfied customer, don't you? If your customer says "Yes" — sure, you sold him the extra accommodation or whatever, but the customer wants it, or sees the advantage in having you make the arrangements or he wouldn't have said yes.

184

Ask the customer what he wants to do and see. Probe a little bit. Certainly you're interested in the customer — it's all a part of getting to know him, his interests, likes and dislikes, his habits, his hobbies, all the things he *values*.

No one will be offended when you ask for the business. Be clear. Be open. Certainly you always make sure your client knows what he's going to get and how much it will cost. Let the client judge the value of what you suggest.

The point is, don't knock it until you've carefully considered all possibilities for direct sales.

Telephone Sales

You are not getting your money's worth out of your telephone unless you are using it for the important sales tool it is. Too frequently outgoing or solicitation sales calls are the last to be made.

If this is the case in your agency, that is, "We do make telephone sales calls whenever we're not busy," then ask yourself why.

Is it because you or your employees don't like making "cold" calls? Be honest. Many people don't, feeling such calls are an intrusion. The real reason is usually that they've not been trained in this technique, which is quite different from handling incoming sales calls. If this is the case, avail yourself of one of the sales training courses given by principals which includes telephone sales.

Airlines, wholesalers, magazines and others are anxious to provide coupons or leads to you. These are either inquiries that have come directly to them, or coupons clipped from ads. Unfortunately, not all are good leads, usually because they are late. But others do a good job. It won't take you long to recognize which principals you want to work with on lead follow-up. One clue: the best ones will be the most demanding in terms of a report or follow-up requirement by a stated time.

Your local newspaper is another good lead source for making calls. Engagements usually signify travel plans. So does a company's moving plans, or executive changes. Call-backs are another type of call often neglected. Often clients appreciate it.

We don't suggest that you simply call at random from the telephone book. But we do suggest that outgoing solicitation calls should be a part of your plan.

Like other sales activities, a simple record should be kept so you know how productive it has been.

Specific times should be set aside for outgoing calls, allowing you to expand your "territory." This doesn't mean the calls shouldn't be made at other times if your people aren't busy. But if the calls aren't scheduled, they probably won't be made.

Direct Mail

A good mailing list can be one of your best sales sources and most effective sales tools. Good lists can be had for as little as $30 per thousand names. On the other hand, a list of Rotarians can probably be had by being a member of Rotary. Again, this is not intended to be a primer on direct mail, but here are a few general considerations.

If you are small, you'll probably keep your list on cards and type the names on envelopes. If you're larger, you'll find it more efficient to use metal or plastic plates. At this point, you may want to contact a local direct mail house. Talk over your situation with them and see what they can do for you. It may save you both dollars and time.

Don't be satisfied with simply a list of past customers, although a satisfied past customer is most likely to respond again. Look for other lists — they are available for rental by every conceivable category. Chosen carefully, they can be a profitable investment.

Another way to develop the list is to ask good customers for the names of friends who might like to receive up-to-date information about travel such as regular newsletters.

Teachers, college students, doctors, members of organizations that hold conventions, people about to retire, are all good candidates for a mailing list, and so is almost everyone who writes or telephones the agency.

Increasingly, magazines are offering to cooperate on programs involving either coupon returns or subscription lists by zip code. Some airlines and other principals have mailing programs which they will make available to you.

Before you remove anyone from a mailing list for suspected lack of interest, it's usually a good idea to send a letter giving him an opportunity to tell you whether he wants to be removed.

To do the job, *any* direct mail piece should be timely, it should show the customer *in his terms* that what you are offering will benefit him. Finally, it should require him to take action, such as returning a coupon showing interest.

One of the most effective direct mail pieces, believe it or not, is still the personal letter. It can do the job often where a fancy folder will fall flat! But it must be personal — not a "Dear Sir" type.

A letter also has the advantage of being the least expensive form of direct mail and at the same time the most flattering provided it is written simply and sincerely, as though the agent is writing to a friend.

While brevity is always desirable, be sure you tell your full story. There's nothing wrong with a letter that runs more than one page, *if* that length is necessary to tell the story.

Don't be gimmicky. Follow the same techniques you would in a sales call. Gain the reader's attention, arouse his interest in your product, tell him how it will benefit *him* (remember you're talking to a selected audience) and ASK FOR THE BUSINESS.

Go back and take a look at your earlier analysis of customer groups and products. On which ones will you make a direct mail effort?

Display

If you have a location that is visible to passing traffic, either vehicular or pedestrian, display is obviously important.

But display doesn't stop there. It's just as important *after* you've lured the prospect into your den. Can he browse? Do counter cards, posters, decor suggest travel ideas to him? Does your office layout do anything to presell him? (See Chapter 2, Office Layout and Design.)

And there are possibilities away from your place of business (billboards, for example). Your place of business is competing with every other storefront on the street. Go out and look at it. Take someone with you. How does it compare?

Does it invite people in? Does it clearly state what you have to sell? Is it attractive and up to date? Does it look warm and inviting on a cold winter's day, or cool in the summer?

How many windows do you have? How close does the traffic pass? Is it automobiles or pedestrian?

All this has to do with how large your display needs to be. As with billboards, if you're trying to get your message across to someone in an automobile, your message must be shorter for reading. If, on the other hand, your traffic is shoppers on foot, you can use more intricate displays to capture their interest.

Select and schedule your displays for those most likely to see them. Schedule them in advance as part of your plan.

Advertising

Will you use newspaper advertising, club publications, sporting events programs, radio spots, or any of the other enticing possibilities? A friendly warning. Advertising can be very effective, providing the message and the media are carefully thought out.

Large display ads are not necessary. You probably can't afford them anyway. A well placed one- or two-inch ad repeated often, telling the public what you do and how to contact you can be very effective. This can cost as little as $6 in a city of 120,000 population.

The Yellow Pages are an excellent medium.

There will be times when you will want to advertise a specific tour or destination package. This will usually be in cooperation with a wholesaler or operator. In this case you'll want to include a coupon with a "key" or code to identify the publication so that later you can measure results. In measuring results, don't rely completely on conversion to sales.

The customer's decision to buy from you is influenced by several factors. It may be that a friend told him you'd done a good job, he was reminded of you by your sign on a bus stop bench, and his wife saw your specific offering in the newspaper.

Radio spots are useful, particularly if they are supported by placement adjacent to a program that suggests travel. Spots sell for as little as $10, again, depending upon the station's coverage, time of day, and frequency of use. Remember, too, that disc jockeys can be strong salesmen as tour conductors on a 1-for-15 basis.

We realize the demands on your time. But several agents in smaller communities have had good success with radio programs of their own,

188

or newspaper columns on travel. People are interested in travel; it makes interesting copy. If you have that creative bent, the column or program can be very effective.

Another possibility is bill stuffers. Many stores will allow you to place a stuffer in their customer statement mailings either at cost or for a small fee. It's an inexpensive means of keeping your name in front of your public.

The simple fact is that you must explore every possible way of keeping your name before the public. It's been proven many times that no matter how familiar someone is with you, he may not think of you when he needs you most. Hence, the need for repetitive reminders.

Finally, in advertising, like any other kind of selling, put yourself in the place of the person you're trying to sell — talk *his* language, describe benefits that are meaningful to him, things he will value.

Promotion

These can be tie-ins with other retailers, such as department stores, or with local newspapers, radio or TV stations, civic organizations. They can be joint efforts with your travel agent colleagues. For example, for several years, the Seattle Chapter of ASTA has been successfully sponsoring, together with a local newspaper, a travel film festival. They have filled the Opera House, made a modest profit from admissions, and most important, have exposed their products to thousands of potential customers.

Most of the carriers, hotel representatives and others produce promotional materials and tools, ranging from printed matter to films. Again, find out what's available and make a list.

Perhaps a touring native group can be commandeered to do a one-hour or less tie-in promotion for their homeland in front of your agency. Hula dancers from Hawaii, a steel band from Trinidad, or a Flamenco dancer from Español are possibilities. Similarly, tulips or cheese from the Netherlands can be displayed. You get the idea.

Thoughtfully and selectively distributed flowers, sea shells, and fruit or foreign handicrafts make remembered give-aways.

Before we go full circle in our marketing cycle, there are a few more topics to cover in the relationship of travel products to customers.

Pricing

To increase profits for factors within your control, do you seek volume, low commission business, or do you seek the more limited high ticket business? Do you add service charges to all service or just selected services? How much service charge? At what point does the addition of service charge or mark-up increase have the result of decreased customer interest in purchasing travel from you?

Difficult questions. Marketing related. Part of your plan and strategy if you care to include pricing alternatives.

Suffice it to say, policy decisions have to be made with the customer in mind. Commissions, mark-ups, and service charges are payment for your time. They pay your bills and feed your family, but economics and the free enterprise system discourage you from providing too much time or service if the customer won't thank you in cash payment for your efforts. It can also be a mistake not to charge enough, or in some cases, not charging what the traffic will bear. Keeping your ears open (a kind of research), and your customer and competition in mind, you will probably do a fine job in pricing/profit.

Suppliers

Viewed from the suppliers' point of view, the travel agent is a sales outlet, the last stop in the distribution channel of products not sold direct. From your viewpoint of course, suppliers are key because they more than anyone affect the price and products of what you offer to the ultimate customer. It's an important partnership in marketing to be considered carefully.

The airlines in particular are recognizing they can no longer say to the travel agent, "You develop the business, and we'll pay you a commission." Instead they, and others, are realizing that a wide array of strong and independent sales outlets — travel agents — are essential to their own growth.

Wholesalers and tour operators, as well as the shipping lines, have, in most cases, recognized the travel agent's role, since they don't sell direct, having the travel agent as their only customer.

Throughout this chapter, we're suggesting that you be selective. This is particularly true in the case of suppliers. Some are easier to work with than others, some produce better products. Some pay better commissions.

Since most wholesalers or tour operators specialize to some extent (areas, special interest, cost, etc.) you probably need to work with several. But you needn't work with all.

How do you find the right ones?

One way is to ask the carrier you find most helpful whom they work with or recommend.

Another is to ask other agents in your community, ASTA, or the Tour Operators Association.

There are four general questions that you should try to answer before working with a particular wholesaler.

1. What kind of business does he run? This isn't just the dollars and cents of financial stability, although that's part of it. You naturally need to know if the wholesaler is financially stable, if he pays his bills to hotels and other operators promptly. You also have to find out how quickly legitimate refunds are paid. Finding out about his business means determining the areas he specializes in, the types of clients he caters to and becoming acquainted with his staff. Does the staff know the area by firsthand experience? Is the staff cooperative, can you rely on their information, or will you have to keep doublechecking their work?

2. Find out if the wholesaler's prices are competitive, and if the wholesaler has good buying power which will mean good value when the tour's components are broken down individually.

3. What about your commissions and the protection of those commissions? Find out about bonus commissions for volume business (another good reason for being selective), and the ease of receiving your additional commissions if your client buys extra commissionable services while on his trip or decides to stay for a longer period.

4. What about sales activity support? The wholesaler's brochures should be not only very clear and specific, but attractive sales pieces as well. Also, the wholesaler should take extra care to make sure that your identity is protected on all correspondence

and vouchers. Find out if the wholesaler helps create a demand for his own tours through advertising and promotion. This kind of effort could make your selling job easier and more profitable. Also find out if he is willing to contribute to your promotional advertising budget by providing ad mats, point-of-purchase display material or participation in advertising costs. You should look for assistance from the wholesaler in other ways, too. He should be able to arrange individual or group familiarization tours to an area at special agent's rates, and he should help educate you and your staff in selling a particular tour or area.

The same principles hold true for others you represent who provide the products to your client. Be selfishly selective — for your client as well as for yourself.

Your Marketing Plan

Now, from all of the above, construct your plan. Decide what is best, and when, in terms of *profit*. Review carefully the other chapters in this book, particularly Chapter 5 on costs and budgets.

We have referred to the plan several times earlier, but let's here review its importance and reassemble the major pieces.

Your plan should represent a series of programs with dollar goals in which all of your merchandising efforts are targeted against specific audiences for specific periods. It should be the best possible relation of costs (including time) to revenues.

With the key parts and actionable elements in mind, you should now make up your own plan. We said earlier it needn't be elaborate. It should, however, contain the following elements.

> *A time period.* At least three calendar months, at most a year. Against the calendar, you should plan:
> —The customer groups you've selected. These may be general such as commercial, singles, families, or specific such as a student class, country club, Rotary Club.
> —The products you intend to sell. Destinations, specific tours, or whatever. The number of sales of each that you believe you can sell.
> —An estimate of the gross revenues these sales will produce and

where. Don't overlook incremental income from insurance or other special services.

Your margin on the above (commission, mark-up, etc.).

Month-by-month, your action — what you intend to do to make those sales. All the things we mentioned earlier such as mailings, advertising, sales calls, promotions. The cost of these.

What we are suggesting is a simple budget of your time, income and selling costs. Those, when related to your other costs as described in Chapter 5, become your marketing plan.

But be flexible; it's not etched in stone. As conditions change, so must you. Don't be too discouraged if your initial plan doesn't work as well as you'd like — those of some of the largest corporations don't.

The important thing is that you've started operating with a plan. Each time you do another, it will be better, because you'll grow increasingly self-critical.

Follow-Up and Follow-Through

When the planned-for period is concluded, measure the results obtained against the plan you made. Examine the performance above and below goals. Try to determine why the differences occurred and what changes are necessary for the next period. Then, make the changes!

Along with your agency sales report forms, and your standard budget and accounting forms enumerated in Chapter 5, you have all the paper work you need. Except for the plan which you now know you have to do anyway, no new paper work has been added. And perhaps you now have an increased appreciation for "all of the paper work" as a logical, coordinated business system. (All thanks to taking the customer's point of view toward your business — marketing!)

Let's get back to the customer. There are other forms of follow-up and there are other benefits. Follow-up serves to bring you up to date on new developments outside as well as inside your agency.

If big ticket customers haven't called lately, or since returning from that special tour, *you* call for the follow-up report. The opinions of your clients, whether good or bad, are a vital measure of the job you're doing, and the key to repeat sales.

If your customer was not completely satisfied, the follow-up allows you to make amends and take appropriate action. It gives the initiative to you, rather than to the customer.

If your customer was satisfied, he may know others who would like a similar trip.

Showing interest in your client after his return gives him the opportunity to participate in the "remembrance after" mentioned earlier. He may be willing to talk to other prospective clients about it, or show slides — word-of-mouth advertising, the most effective kind of any in this business of travel.

Follow-up can be done by letter or telephone. The important thing is to do it.

Re-Cap

You can run your business profitably, but to do so requires more than just handling the day-to-day business. It is at the travel agency that all the parts of the travel product come together — the *total* product, not only the obvious, such as transportation, sightseeing and accommodations, but all the services of travel which combine to make a total travel experience.

You must take the initiative. Seek assistance from those you represent. Spend the time to learn more about these people who are not your customers but who might be. Know what they value. Plan what will happen, don't simply let it happen.

Train yourself and your staff not to be satisfied with a sale of transportation and a hotel room. Find out what the customer wants to do when he gets there, so that he leaves your agency with extra commissionable coupons in his pocket.

Profitability requires your adopting a policy of not letting a prospect go without a sale. Rather, sell him something he'll enjoy, even if the sale may be smaller than you'd like. Do a good job for him, so that you can sell him more next year. Travel is a step-by-step business. The family you sell on a U.S. resort this year may well be ready for Europe next. People who have been to Europe may be ready for the Orient. People who have taken a motor coach tour in Europe may be ready for car rental.

It would be naive to suggest that, with today's industry structure and remuneration scale, profit comes easily. It would be just as naive to expect things to change overnight, or to wait for changes over which you have no control.

But you *are* going to see enormous change in the next few years. You are in the travel agency industry at a time when the principals and suppliers are seriously beginning to realize the value of good retail agents. They are beginning to compete for the dollars you can produce. They are anxious to help. Some are more able than others. You should decide which can be most helpful to you, go to them and jointly decide how you can do the best job for your customers at the best available return to you.

This can be done profitably only by truly trying to understand the customer and doing your best to look at your agency and its products from the customer's point of view. That's the essence of marketing in this "people" business.

Chapter 9

Legal Considerations in Travel Agency Management

by

Paul S. Quinn

As a travel agent, you are one of innumerable independent businessmen in the United States. Legal considerations of which you must be aware fall into two general categories: first, those which confront you as a businessman and second, those which confront you as a businessman specifically engaged in the travel agency industry.

In the first category are such considerations as the basic legal structure of your company, contractual and other obligations to your employees and other persons with whom you deal on a commercial basis, compliance with federal wage and hour laws and similar matters. In the second category are both legal considerations which grow out of your relationship with principals who supply travel and related services and your legal obligations to the public.

This section of the book will focus on some general considerations which confront all businessmen operating in the United States today. We will discuss various types of business organization available, with a description of the characteristics and advantages and disadvantages of

197

each. We will also examine the existing provisions of the federal wage and hour laws and discuss the obligations which they impose on you as an employer.

The balance of this section will concern legal considerations which specifically confront travel agents, such as the legal structure of the travel agency industry, the role of the airline conferences, and the legal influences of the CAB and other government agencies. Also examined will be the obligations which you, as a travel agent, have in your dealings with carriers and the traveling public.

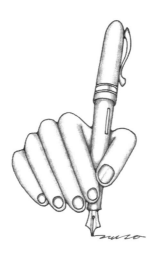

Principal Forms of Business Organization

The first problem confronting anyone in the travel agency industry is the choice of a form of business organization. Many diverse factors are relevant to this decision. These include tax treatment, continuity of existence, centralization of management, liability of the owner, transferability of interest, ability to amass capital over a period of time, access to new capital, ability of the enterprise to acquire, hold, and dispose of property, ability of the enterprise to sue and be sued as an entity, state fees and license requirements, application of state and federal securities laws, and expense involved in setting up the desired form.

The most common forms of business organization used in the United States are the sole proprietorship, partnership, limited partnership, and corporation. Each of these, as applied to a prospective travel agent, will be discussed in turn.

Sole Proprietorship

The sole proprietorship is the simplest business form of all, as it does not involve the association of separate parties. As an unincorporated enterprise, it has no existence apart from that of the proprietor, who is in sole managerial control and who accepts unlimited liability.

Income from the business is treated as personal income to the proprietor, and losses, if incurred in the early years, can be offset against other personal income. However, as the enterprise grows and becomes more successful, the application of high individual tax rates makes the accumulation of capital from within the business difficult, and the access of an individual to new capital is likely to be limited. In order to sustain the growth of his business, the sole proprietor often finds it necessary to associate with others in a partnership and/or to incorporate.

Partnership

The partnership is the simplest form in which different parties can associate for the purpose of carrying on a business for profit. Like the sole proprietorship, it has no existence apart from that of its owners. The rights and obligations of the parties to the partnership is a matter of contract, determined by the terms of the partnership agreement.

Partnerships are governed in nearly all states by the Uniform Partnership Act. This Act provides a vehicle for establishing the rights and obligations of the partners in situations where the partnership agreement is silent. It also establishes certain principles under which all partnerships must operate, the partnership agreement to the contrary notwithstanding. One such principle is that each partner is individually liable for partnership obligations to the full extent of his individual assets.

Among the advantages offered by a partnership are the informal manner in which it may be formed and conducted, the general absence of state fees and filing requirements, and taxation at individual rates, which avoids the double taxation attendant to the corporate form and which allows partners to write off the losses likely to occur in the early years of a venture against other personal income. However, as in the case of a sole proprietorship, growth may be retarded by the imposition of high individual tax rates which make the accumulation of capital from within the business difficult. This consideration and others often lead to the decision to incorporate.

Limited Partnership

The limited partnership is universally recognized in the United States and is usually governed by the Uniform Limited Partnership Act. With but few exceptions, general partnership principles apply as well to the limited partnership. A limited partnership requires at least one general partner who has unlimited liability and any number of limited partners who are liable only to the extent of the capital contribution required of them. The filing of a certificate of limited partnership is required by the state in which the limited partnership is to operate, which puts potential creditors on notice that at least one of the partners has limited liability. The price paid by the limited partner for his limited liability is the prohibition against his having any voice in management, at peril of his being held liable as a general partner.

Corporation

The corporation is a legal entity separate and apart from its shareholders, which is organized under the corporation law of the state or states in which it is incorporated. There is no federal corporation law, although many activities of corporations engaged in interstate commerce are, of course, governed by federal statute. The corporate form is the most popular for enterprises of any size, largely because of tax and liability advantages to the shareholder-owners.

Corporations are taxed as a legal entity, but any dividends distributed to shareholders are taxed again to the shareholders at individual rates, and since the corporate rate for large incomes is much lower than the individual rate, the corporation is the most advantageous vehicle for the accumulation of capital form within the business. Corporations also have greater access than any other type of enterprise to both public and private capital markets. It should be noted that shareholders of corporations which meet the requirements of Sub-chapter S of the Internal Revenue Code may elect to be taxed individually as if the income were earned directly by them, i.e. taxed as partners or, in the case of a single shareholder, as a sole proprietor. One advantage of this approach is the ability to write off any losses from corporate operations against other personal income.

The other great advantage of the corporate form is the limitation on the liability of the shareholders to the amount of their investment. This is true even if all the stock is held by one shareholder. It should be noted, however, that a court may pierce the corporate veil, thus holding the shareholder or shareholders individually liable to the full extent of their personal assets, if the corporate privilege is abused to the detriment of creditors or the general public.

The process of incorporation prescribed by the typical state corporation statute is relatively simple. Today's corporation statute is, in effect, an enabling act which is designed to make corporate operations easy from the management standpoint. A specified number of incorporators, usually three, must sign a certificate of incorporation, which contains information required by the statute. This document must be filed with the Secretary of State, who will usually issue a certificate stating that the statute has been complied with. Upon such filing, the enterprise will usually constitute a corporation. In addition to this filing, further registration and fees may be required in order to do business in other states. Registration under federal security laws and state "Blue Sky" laws is required upon the public subscription of any corporate security.

A distinction is made in fact, although generally not in law, between public issue corporations, shares of which are held by a large number of persons and traded in public markets, and close corporations, shares of which are held by either a single person or a small group of persons and not actively traded. Most incorporated travel agencies are of the close corporation type, although the future will undoubtedly see more and more of the larger agencies "going public."

Although the state corporation statute usually governs both close and public issue corporations, regulation of close corporations is in a state of flux. The clear trend is toward allowing close corporations greater flexibility in their internal affairs than is possible under the general corporation laws, which were written with large public issue corporations in mind. This liberalization has come about in several ways, from court decisions applying the terms of the general corporation law to the close corporation situation, to amendment of the general corporation law, to the passage, in a few states, of entirely separate statutes governing the close corporation. The trend of these changes is toward treating close corporations for what they really are, incorporated partnerships. To varying degrees, they allow managerial control to be vested directly in the shareholders rather than indirectly through the board of directors elected by the shareholders. Such steps which simplify operation of a close corporation make it a much more attractive alternative for the operation of a travel agency by a small businessman.

The Federal Wage and Hour Laws as Applied to the Travel Agent

Travel agents are, in most instances, subject to the wage and hour provisions of the Fair Labor Standards Act of 1938, as amended. The sections which follow summarize the application of the Act to travel agents.

I. *Wage amd Hour Requirements* — The Act establishes a minimum wage for most workers, and requires that employees be paid time-and-a-half for all hours in excess of 40 worked in any one work week, regardless of the time worked in prior or subsequent work weeks. The unit of measure is always the work week, but there is no requirement that it begin on any specific day of the week. Time-and-a-half is computed on the basis of the employee's actual wage, which includes all compensation to which he is entitled, including any commissions or mandatory performance bonuses.

II. *Consequences of Violation of the Act* — Consequences for even unintentional violations of the Act can be severe. In addition to being liable to their employees or former employees for any unpaid minimum wages or earned overtime, employers may also be liable for an equal amount as "liquidated damages." The Act provides that the Secretary of Labor, at the request of an employee, may bring suit on behalf of that employee or all employees to recover such damages. Although the Secretary cannot recover liquidated damages on behalf of the employee, he is entitled to receive interest on the amount recovered plus the cost of bringing suit. Federal courts have the power to issue injunctions against employers to require that back wages and overtime payments to employees be paid. The Act also imposes criminal penalties on employers who are found to have intentionally violated the Act. These penalties range up to a $10,000 fine and/or a six month prison sentence for second offenses.

III. *Covered Employees* — All employees of a travel agency will be subject to the minimum wage and overtime provisions of the Act, unless they qualify for exemption as "executive" or "administrative" employees.

In order to qualify for exemption as an "executive" employee under the latest regulations, the person in question must: (1) be paid a salary of at least $125 per week; (2) have as his *primary duty* the management of the agency or of a recognized department or subdivision thereof; (3) customarily and regularly direct the work of at least two other employees; (4) have authority to hire, fire, and promote other employees, or to strongly influence such decisions (this requirement is excused if he makes at least $200 per week); (5) be able to exercise his own discretion in his work, and; (6) spend less than 20 per cent of his time on non-executive type work, unless he is in sole charge of an establishment or branch or owns at least a 20 per cent interest in the agency.

The term "administrative" employee contemplates an executive assistant or the like, not someone who spends most of his time performing clerical duties. He must: (1) be paid a salary of at least $125 per week; (2) perform office or nonmanual work directly related to management policies or general business operations of his employer or employer's customers; (3) customarily and regularly exercise independent discretion and judgment in his work; (4) either work as an assistant to an executive or proprietor, or work solely on special assignments with only general supervision, or solely in technical or specialized areas with only general supervision; (5) not devote more than 20 per cent of his work week to other "nonadministrative" duties. If the employee makes at least $200 per week the only qualifications necessary are that his work be of office or non-manual type, that it relate directly to management policies or general business operations of his employer or employer's customers, and that it require him to use his own discretion and judgment.

IV. *Work Outside the United States* — the Act covers only employees working in the United States, its territories and possessions. Therefore, for any week that an employee such as a tour escort works outside of the United States, he is not covered by the Act, and his employer is not required to pay him the minimum wage and time-and-a-half for overtime. One caveat should be noted. The employee is only exempted from coverage if he has worked the *entire* work week in question outside of the United States. If he works *any part* of a particular work week in the United States, its territories, or possessions, that work week is covered, and he must be paid the minimum wage and any overtime for the entire week.

V. *Keeping of Records* — Records must be kept for all employees, including name, address and salary. The employer need not keep records of hours worked or a breakdown of hourly compensation for bona fide executive or administrative employees, or for employees whose entire work week is spent outside of the United States. If, however, there is any possibility that a question might arise as to whether such an employee's time was covered, it would be to the travel agent's advantage to have detailed records available.

VI. *Employee vs. Independent Contractor* — The Act applies only to "employees," not "independent contractors." An "employee," however, cannot become an "independent contractor" by merely signing a contract to that effect. If his services are rendered as an integral part of the travel agent's business and are performed pursuant to a permanent arrangement under the travel agent's direct supervision, he will generally be held to be an employee. If a particular arrangement did not offer a purported independent contractor substantial opportunities for profit or loss, did not call for him to exercise a great deal of initiative, judgment or foresight, he would also be considered an employee.

VII. *Voluntary After Hours Work by Employees* — The employer must pay overtime to employees who voluntarily work after hours even if they are not requested to do so by the firm. Management has the obligation of either exercising control to see that there is no overtime work or of compensating the employee for such work.

VIII. *Attendance at Social Events* — An employee's attendance at business cocktail parties or other such social events will be considered working time unless: (1) Attendance is outside the employee's regular working hours; (2) Attendance is voluntary (it is not voluntary where required by the employer or where the employee is lead to believe that his present working conditions would be adversely affected by non-attendance); (3) The event is not directly related to the employee's job; (4) The employee does not perform any productive work during such attendance.

IX. *Employees' Time Spent After Hours in Educational Activities* — If an employee is required by his employer to study or otherwise engage in educational activities, that time must be compensated and is also subject to the overtime provisions of the Act. If, on the other hand, the employee's participation in such activities is voluntary and not related to his job and if there is no direct benefit to the employer from time so spent, the time need not be compensated.

If an employee voluntarily takes courses offered by his employer for the purpose of developing higher skills and in preparation for advancement to a higher skilled position, then the training is not considered to be directly related to his job. However, if the purpose for such study or training is to improve the employee's efficiency or productivity in his present position, the training is considered to be directly related to his job and such time must be compensated.

If an employee attends an independent school, college or trade school on his own initiative, the time so spent is not considered time worked for his employer, even if the courses taken relate to his job.

X. *Familiarization Trips* — Time spent on familiarization trips is subject to the minimum wage and overtime requirements of the Act where the trip occurs during the employee's regular working hours and is undertaken at the employer's request. If such a trip is taken during vacation time, it is only covered if the employer requires it or leads the employee to believe that his opportunities for advancement or his present working conditions will be adversely affected if he fails to make the trip. If the employer pays the expenses of an employee on the trip and requires submission of a report, it may be difficult to argue that it is merely a voluntary vacation trip and not work done for the benefit of the employer.

XI. *Discrimination in Employment on the Basis of Sex or Age* — Under the Act, employers may not discriminate financially between men and women whose jobs require equal skills, effort, and responsibility, and which are performed under similar working conditions. Further, it is unlawful under the Age Discrimination in Employment Act for a firm employing 25 or more persons to discriminate in any way against any person between 40 and 65 years of age.

Two caveats should be noted. The first is that the law is subject to change both as to minimum permissible wages and scope of coverage, so the travel agent must keep himself abreast of developments in the law. The other is that the wage and hour laws are but one example of many federal and state laws of which travel agents must be aware and with which they must comply. Other such laws include tax statutes and regulations, anti-discrimination provision of the Civil Rights Act, workmen's compensation laws, anti-trust laws and truth-in-lending requirements.

The Legal Structure of the Travel Agency Industry

Although the travel agency industry is not a regulated industry as such, agents are subject to extensive control over their operating procedures and practices. This is attributable to the fact that air transportation, the sale of which is the mainstay of a travel agent's business, is an industry regulated by the Federal Aviation Act of 1958 (the Act). The Act established the Civil Aeronautics Board and imposed

206

upon the Board the duty to assure that the country has a safe, efficient and economic air transportation system.

The Civil Aeronautics Board, in order to accomplish this Congressional mandate, has the authority to exempt agreements among air carriers from the operation of the anti-trust laws. Prominent among such agreements are those pertaining to travel agents entered into by the international air carriers through the International Air Transport Association, and the domestic air carriers through the Air Traffic Conference of America.

IATA and ATC Regulations

As an appointed travel agent you should be familiar with the basic provisions of IATA Resolution 810 (a) — the Passenger Sales Agency Rules, and those additional resolutions set forth in the handbook issued by IATA entitled, "IATA Resolution Applicable to Approved Sales Agents." Likewise, you should be familiar with ATC Resolution 80.10 and those related resolutions set forth in the ATC Agents' Handbook.

The sales agency resolutions of IATA and ATC are considered agreements among air carriers affecting air transportation under the terms of Section 412 of the Act. They must be submitted in writing to the CAB and the CAB has an obligation either to approve or disapprove them. Once the Board approves an agreement either as submitted or with modifications, anti-trust immunity is extended to that agreement. The terms of those agreements are built into the contractual obligations, with IATA and ATC carriers, as appropriate, which the travel agent assumes and by which he is bound in his dealings with the carriers.

Since you have already established your qualifications to serve as an approved travel agent, your primary concern with respect to the provisions of the sales agency agreements relate to compliance with the provisions of the agreements in your day-to-day operating functions, and the rights available to you in the event that it is alleged that you have violated one or more of the provisions of the agreements.

It is important at the outset to keep in mind that under Paragraph 1 of both the IATA and ATC sales agency agreements the effectiveness of the agreements is contingent upon the delivery of a certificate of appointment by an individual carrier to you as a travel agent. Once this certificate of appointment has been executed, the agreement becomes operative and the provisions of Paragraph 2 of the agreement which define the scope of your authority as an agent representing the carrier come into play. Under the agreement, you are required to act in accordance with the carrier's rules, regulations and instructions.

There are strict requirements imposed in the agreement with respect to the keeping of records and provisions for the inspection of records. For example, Paragraph 5 of the ATC agreement requires that you must retain a duplicate copy of each sales report and of all supporting documents required under the agreement for a period of at least two years. You are also required, as an agent, to make books and records relating to the sale of transportation offered by the carrier open to inspection by a carrier representative. Neither agreement specifies which books and records must be made available for inspection. It can be assumed that a carrier has the right to inspect only those books and records which relate to the sale of transportation by the carrier and not matters unrelated to that activity.

Suspension Provisions and Procedures

An agent may be suspended or removed from the approved list of ATC or IATA in the event he ceases to meet the eligibility standards provided for in the resolutions or violates the Sales Agency Agreement. With respect to eligibility standards, the agency committee of each conference has the obligation of determining compliance with minimum requirements. In the case of alleged violations of the sales agency agreement, a compliance panel of the conference has the obligation of determining whether alleged violations exist. Certain infractions by the agent of standards established in the resolutions such as the failure to maintain the required bond or to remit carrier funds in accordance with the agreement can result in automatic removal by the conference. Other alleged infractions of the sales agency agreement can result in the issuance of a complaint by a compliance panel which, in turn, could subject the agent to a reprimand, suspension or removal from the approved list.

Usually compliance panel action results from an investigation by the conference office of enforcement which is empowered to conduct audits of agent's books and records. The enforcement office can request the Executive Secretary to docket a complaint requesting specific sanctions in cases where it appears that an agent is violating an agreement.

Once the Executive Secretary decides to docket a complaint, he will attach a copy of the complaint to a letter advising the agent of the enforcement action and of the right to tender a written response and evidence in support of his version of the alleged infraction within thirty days following receipt of the complaint. The Executive Secretary will then proceed to designate a compliance panel to meet as soon as practical after receipt of the agent's submissions.

The compliance panel consists of three airline employees selected from among a group of airline employees designated by each member of the conference to be available to serve on that panel. The identity of the members of the compliance panel is not made public, the time and place of the hearing is not revealed and, although representatives of the Bureau of Enforcement and attorneys for the ATC may appear before the compliance panel to present their view of the alleged infraction, the agent is not allowed to appear in person or to be represented by counsel during the compliance panel's deliberations.

If the compliance panel finds that the agency engaged in one or more of the alleged infractions the agent is advised of the panel's findings and of the sanctions decided upon by the panel.

The agent can either accept the determination of the compliance panel, which could call for either a reprimand, suspension or removal from the approved list, or can contest such a decision. Should he choose to contest the decision he may, within thirty days following the receipt of the notice of the compliance panel's action, have the matter submitted to a final and binding Board of Arbitration. The Board of Arbitration consists of three individuals, in the case of the ATC: one selected by the Executive Secretary, one by the agent, and a third arbitrator who shall serve as chairman of the tribunal selected by the first two. In IATA the agent has the option of selecting a one man or three man arbitration panel. Arbitration procedures are spelled out in Paragraph 27 of the ATC sales agency agreement and Section H(5) of the IATA Passenger Sales Agent Rules.

It is important, particularly in those instances where an agent is faced with the possibility of suspension or removal from the approved list, that he avail himself of the services of a competent attorney as early as possible in his dispute with the air carriers, preferably as soon as representatives of the Bureau of Enforcement request permission to review his books and records.

Although the sales agency agreements give the enforcement authorities power to review books and records of the agent which relate to the sale of air transportation, it is sometimes helpful to assure that the principal officer of the agency involved be present and review with the representative of the enforcement office material which is to be examined and assure that only the material which pertains to the sale of air transportation be subject to review.

Certain violations of the sales agency agreements are not subject to arbitration. They pertain to the obligations imposed upon the agents to remit three times a month to the area settlement bank, in the case of the ATC sales agency agreement, and twice a month to the members of International Air Transport Association, in the case of the IATA agreement. Failure to make timely remittances can result in automatic removal from the approved list. Therefore, it is essential that you establish and maintain effective procedures to assure strict compliance with the reporting and remittance provisions of the sales agency agreements.

ATC and IATA arbitration proceedings generally grow out of allegations by the carriers of an improper claim of override commissions for the sale of various types of air tours, failure to maintain adequate records to substantiate the sale of tours or the improper use of reduced rate travel privileges. It is most important therefore that you familiarize yourself with the provisions of the sales agency agreement as they pertain to these activities and maintain complete and accurate books and records for the period of time specified by the resolutions.

Ticket Stock Theft and Liability

Another problem area concerns the agent's responsibility in the event that his ticket stock or validating plates are stolen. In June of 1970 the Air Traffic Conference voted to change the provisions of Section 18 of the ATC sales agency agreement which imposed virtually absolute liability on travel agents in the event that the agent had his ticket stock or validating plates stolen. Under the revised language an agent would be responsible to the carriers for the value of the stolen ticket stock only if the agent fails to exercise "reasonable care" regarding his control of the ticket stock and validating plate. The ATC carriers have promulgated guide lines which should be followed by travel agents to assure that the agents' control of these materials amounts to the exercise of "reasonable care."

The assessment of service charges by travel agents raises legal questions also. As a general rule, an agent may not impose a service charge for making reservations or issuing tickets since the agent may not charge a lesser or greater amount for these activities than specified in airline tariffs. However, if an agent performs additional services for the benefit of his client, it is generally proper to impose a reasonable service charge. The agent should, however, clearly advise his client or customer of the assessment of any service charge in advance to avoid misunderstanding or controversy.

Legal Liability of Travel Agents to Their Clients

More and more frequently, travel agents are the objects of law suits brought by travelers disappointed or angered over either an alleged failure on the part of the agent to perform his services properly or, over failure of the carrier, hotel, or other actual provider of a travel service to perform properly. In this latter case, even though the travel agent is generally not at fault, the difficulties encountered by the traveler in ascertaining the proper legal entity which owns the carrier or hotel, or of obtaining jurisdiction over the proper party, make the travel agent, who is likely to be found in the traveler's own locality, an inviting target for litigation. These factors plus the tremendous expansion of the industry and the ever increasing reliance by the public on the services of professional travel agents make it vitally important that you have a working knowledge of your liability to the public.

Categorical statements about the legal responsibility of travel agents to their clients for the proper performance of the travel services and accommodations which they sell are likely to be more misleading than helpful. No detailed legal scheme for such responsibility has yet been laid out by the courts, partly because of the unique structure of the travel industry and partly because there are at present few statutory regulations or licensing requirements covering travel agents. Liability must, therefore, be determined primarily on the basis of common law principles of negligence, agency, and contracts. Uncertainty is inherent in this situation, because of differences in the laws among the various states and because of developing trends in the law, such as increasing activism on the part of many courts in the field of consumer protection. However, even given all these variables, a general knowledge of present law and developing trends is a valuable asset to the travel agent.

Travel Agents' Liability for Their Own Wrongful Actions

Aside from the obvious duty to refrain from the commission of willful and deliberate torts, such as fraudulant misrepresentation, the travel agent's minimum duty to his client is established by the law of negligence. Travel agents have the same duty as everyone else to refrain from conduct which creates an unreasonable risk of harm to others. The travel agent must act as a reasonable and prudent man would act under the circumstances in serving the interests of his client.

At least one authority has speculated that travel agents, because of their presumed expertise, might come to be held to a higher standard of conduct than the typical provider of business services. Under such a view, the travel agent like a doctor or a lawyer, would be held to a high standard of care and skill. Weighing heavily against the application of such a "malpractice" standard is the fact that travel agents are not presently required to undergo either formal training or examination as to competence. However, as industry efforts to increase professionalism proceed, and if the state or federal governments establish minimum standards of competence, the possibility that travel agents will be held to a standard of conduct as professionals increases.

Travel Agents' Liability for the Failure of Carriers, Hotels, or Other Providers of Travel Services to Perform Properly

Whether, and if so, to what extent, the travel agent will be liable to his clients for the failure of the actual supplier of the travel service or accommodation to perform adequately will depend to a large extent on

212

the facts in any given case. Of special importance is clarification of the facts — can the travel agent be held to be acting as agent for the provider of the service on the one hand or the client on the other? Confusion on this point exists because a travel agent generally acts as a broker in bringing two contracting parties together, and because the interests of the travel agent are not completely merged or separated from those of the supplier of travel services.

It may happen that a court will find the travel agent to be agent for both the client and the actual provider of the services in different phases of his operation. In most cases, the courts have simply assumed without extensive analysis that the travel agent has acted as agent for the provider of the travel service involved. In some instances, however, it is clear that the travel agent acts as agent for the client, and the finding of such a relationship greatly increases the scope of the travel agent's liability to the client. Also, because the travel agent retains many attributes of an independent businessman, he may be found not to be acting as agent for either party, in which case his liability is determined on the basis of contractual obligations to his client.

In most circumstances it seems clear that a travel agent will continue to be regarded as an agent for the carriers or other principals whose services he sells. The clearest such situation is the appointment of a travel agent in writing by a carrier pursuant to a carrier conference approved sales agency agreement. The same result would attach where travel agents arrange charters or sell cruises on non-conference affiliated carriers. In such cases, although there is no conference approved sales agency agreement, and there may be no express agreement between the carrier and the travel agent at all, the carrier contracts for the agent's services by offering brochures or other materials which indicate a commitment, prior to any dealing by the agents with the client, to pay the travel agent a commission for any bookings. The travel agent in such a situation looks to the carrier as his sole source of compensation. It is desirable in such circumstances for the agent to have an understanding in writing with the carrier spelling out the exact role he is to play.

Although the travel agent's relationship with a hotel is less clear, it seems likely that he will be held to be acting as agent for the hotel on the basis of an implied agency. While no express agency agreement

213

exists, surrounding circumstances, such as the fact that the travel agent looks to the hotel for payment of his commission, show that an agency relationship exists. The case for finding such an agency is strengthened where the travel agent clearly indicates to the client that he is acting as a representative of the hotel.

As a general rule, where the travel agent is found to be the agent of a carrier or hotel, he is not personally liable to the client because the client is really contracting with the principal, the carrier or hotel. However, the agent loses his immunity and becomes personally liable for his principal's failure to perform where he guarantees the principal's performance, e.g., guarantees that a hotel will honor a reservation; when he acts without authority, e.g., sells confirmed space in a hotel under the mistaken belief that he has the authority to do so, and the hotel refuses to honor the "reservation;" where he does not disclose to the client that he is acting on behalf of a principal rather than on his own behalf; or even where he discloses that a principal exists but does not disclose the principal's identity.

In the undisclosed or partially-disclosed principal situation there is a special caution. Courts vary in the extent to which they will take note of the fact that most people know that a travel agent is not the owner or operator of the services which can be purchased through him. They also differ in their determination of what constitutes adequate disclosure. Some courts hold that it is sufficient to disclose the principal's identity so that a reasonable man would know that there is a principal and who the principal is. Other courts hold that the mere disclosure of the principal's trade name is not sufficient where the carrier or hotel is incorporated under another name, because in such a case the client is left with an unreasonably harsh burden of unraveling the ownership puzzle for purposes of suit. To be completely safe on this point, full and complete disclosure should be made in writing by the agent to the client at the time the contract is entered into.

Agent of the Client

Although no reported cases so hold, it is likely that in some circumstances a travel agent could be held to be the agent of the client. Such a situation might arise where the travel agent assembles a Foreign Independent Tour (FIT) for a client, holding himself out to the client as possessing special expertise in the field, tailoring the tour to the client's specifications, receiving part of his remuneration from the client, and generally working under the client's direction. In the case of package tours, which are offered to a client on a "take it or leave it" basis in which the agent does not work under the detailed direction of the client, and which are sold pursuant to a written sales agency agreement with a carrier, it is less likely that a travel agent would be held to be an agent for the client.

Where the travel agent is held to be the agent of the client, his duties toward the client are substantially increased. He owes the client the fiduciary duties which every agent owes to his principal: the exercise of reasonable care and skill, the highest degree of faith and loyalty, and disclosure to the client-principal of all relevant information coming to the agent's knowledge. The disclosure requirement dictates not only that the agent avoid actual misrepresentation, but also that he disclose all facts and difficulties known to him which involve risk to the comfort and safety of the client, e.g., an affirmative duty to warn the client about booking with a hotel which he knows or suspects has a conscious policy of overbooking.

Contractual Liability

Even if no agency is found to exist, the travel agent may still be held liable to his client on the basis of the contractual relationship between them. If the travel agent guarantees a performance or promises to do a specific act, the failure of the guaranteed performance or his failure to do the specific act promised will subject him to contractual liability.

The primary area of uncertainty with respect to a travel agent's contractual liability is the extent to which he will be held to have given an implied warranty that the actual provider of the travel service will perform properly. The present state of the law is that the travel agent does not by implication warrant the results of the performance of the actual provider of the service. However, as the recent trend toward greater consumer protection increases, courts may reject the agency analysis under which travel agents are likely to be relieved of liability and substitute a breach of implied warranty analysis, in the process extending the warranty in the sale of services to the same degree as in the sale of goods, so that travel agents would be held strictly liable for proper performance by the supplier of the actual service. If the law were to develop along these lines, an agent held liable on this theory would have an action for reimbursement against the party primarily at fault.

Disclaimer Clauses

Attempts by travel agents to disclaim liability for non-performance by the actual suppliers of the travel services which they sell are not viewed favorably by the courts. Disclaimer clauses are always construed strictly against the travel agent and are often held invalid for lack of sufficient notice to the client, either because the language used is too vague or because the disclaimer is printed in such a fashion that the client is not likely to see it, e.g., in fine print on the back of tour folders. Other factors relied on by the courts to disallow disclaimer clauses are inequality of bargaining power in favor of the person seeking the protection of the disclaimer and the general view that they are offensive to public policy. While courts in some states may still enforce such clauses, it seems clear that travel agents in the United States will not be able to rely on them in the future with any degree of certainty.

In this section of the book we have attempted to touch upon some of the major considerations which should concern you as a businessman/travel agent. Obviously, the discussion has not been all-inclusive nor was it designed to anticipate the many questions which you may have regarding the legal aspects of your travel agency, but as an attempt to set out some general guidelines. However, we urge that you avail yourselves of the professional advice of an attorney concerning those matters covered in this Chapter, as well as any other questions which might arise in the conduct of your business.

Insurance

In view of the legal exposure or liabilities which you have in your dealings with the carriers and the public, it is well to consider carefully the availability of good insurance coverage which would afford you a degree of protection in your day-to-day business operations. There is available third-party liability insurance, including errors and omissions insurance.

With the increased reliance by the traveling public on the services of travel agents, it is going to become more and more important in the future for the professional travel agent to recognize the extent and scope of his liability to both his carrier principals and the traveling public and to take advantage of professional legal advice involving his business practices and where possible, to obtain insurance coverage to minimize his legal liability and exposure.

Projections

The extent to which countries throughout the world are recognizing the important role played by travel agents in the promotion of travel and tourism was evidenced by an international convention held in April of 1970 in Brussels which led to the adoption of an international treaty on travel agent liability. This treaty has been ratified by several European governments and during the months and years ahead, the 58 governments, including the United States, which participated in the international convention will be giving serious consideration to ratification of this treaty. The treaty attempts to distinguish between the role played by tour operators and retail travel agents in the sale of international travel and tourism and to establish rather precise lines of responsibility on both tour operators and retail agents in their dealings with the public.

The substantial expansion in the sale of charter transportation and the unfortunate charter strandings and defaults by certain organizations promoting charter programs is prompting the Congress to look into proposals which could lead to the establishment of a federal regulatory program over United States travel agents. In addition, certain states are considering legislation which would impose bonding and trust account requirements on some, if not all, persons who offer to sell to the public air transportation. It can be expected that governments at the state, national and international level are going to continue to look into the need for designing new rules and regulations directed at the activities of travel agents.

There is much that can be done by you as a travel agent to justify increased public reliance on your professional services. For example, active participation in a trade association in the travel field gives you an opportunity to help bring about improvements and changes in your business and to shape the important issues which confront your industry.

In addition, you should avail yourselves of the good cooperation offered by the Civil Aeronautics Board through the Board's liaison officer with the travel agency industry. Request for information and advice are welcomed by the CAB on any issues which come within the Board's jurisdiction. By the same token, the staff of IATA and ATC have as part of their responsibility to assist Conference-approved agents in meeting obligations on behalf of the airlines. Do not hesitate to direct inquiries or requests for assistance to the Conferences or the individual airline members of the Conference on any matter which pertains to the sale of air transportation. The same advice applies with respect to the sale of steamship travel and inquiries should be directed to the relevant steamship conference.

In addition to strict legal considerations with respect to the operations of your agency, it is going to become increasingly important for you to upgrade both your own qualifications and those of your employees through participation in either formal or informal educational programs. The Institute of Certified Travel Agents offers an excellent formal educational program designed primarily for you as a travel agent principal. Other educational programs offered by ASTA and individual airlines are well suited to help you upgrade the proficiency and professionalism of your employees.

As a professional travel agent, you are playing a very crucial role in one of the most dynamic phases of this country's and the world's economy — travel and tourism. The importance of the role you play is going to increase in the years ahead and will be accompanied by an increase in the nature and scope of your professional and legal responsibilities. The extent to which you recognize and cope with these responsibilities will, to a large extent, determine your true value both to the traveling public and to the airlines and other principals whom you represent. Better understanding and use of the laws will naturally further your standing and profitability, and prevent embarrassing and financially costly errors.

BIBLIOGRAPHY

Albrook, Robert C., "Why There's So Much Incompetence in Business," *Fortune*, March, 1969.

Aspley, John Cameron, Ed., *The Dartnell Office Administration Handbook*. Chicago; The Dartnell Corporation, 1967.

Broek, Jan O. and John W. Webb, *A Geography of Mankind*, New York; McGraw-Hill Book Company, 1968.

Bureau of Census, Department of Commerce, "Travel Agencies" (BC67SS7) *1967 Census of Business Selected Services*, Washington, D. C.; U. S. Government Printing Office, 1970.

Chruden, Herbert J. and Arthur W. Sherman, Jr., *Personnel Management*, Second Edition, Cincinnati; South Western Publishing Company, 1963.

Chruden, Herbert J. and Arthur W. Sherman, Jr., *Readings in Personnel Management*, Second Edition, Cincinnati; South Western Publishing Company, 1966.

Dale, Ernest, *Management Theory and Practice*, Second Edition, New York; McGraw-Hill Book Company, 1969.

Dalkins, Lola B., *Readings in Office Management*, Boulder, Colorado; Pruett Press, 1967.

Dearden, John F., Warren McFarlan and Philip B. Applewhite, *Management Information Systems*, Homewood, Illinois; Richard D. Irwin, Inc. 1966.

Diebold, John, "What's Ahead in Information Technology," *Harvard Business Review*, September-October, 1965.

219

Greisman, Bernard, Ed., *J. K. Lasser's Business Management Handbook*, Third Edition, New York; McGraw-Hill Book Company, 1968.

Herzberg, Frederick, *Work and the Nature of Man*, New York; The World Publishing Company, 1966.

Hicks, Hubert G., *The Management of Organizations*, New York; McGraw-Hill Book Company, 1967.

Hodge, Bartow and Robert N. Hogson, *Management and the Computer in Information and Control Systems*, New York; McGraw-Hill Book Company, 1969.

Holden, Paul E., Carlton A. Pederson and Gayton E. Germane, *Top Management*, New York; McGraw-Hill Book Company, 1968.

Howell, F. Clark, *Early Man*, New York; Time-Life Books, 1965.

Johnson, H. Webster and William G. Savage, *Administrative Office Management*, Reading, Massachusetts; Addison-Wesley Publishing Company, 1968.

Mayfield, Harold, "Upgrading the Workforce: Don't Overshoot the Mark," *Management Review*, June, 1964.

McCarthy, E. Jerome, *Basic Marketing*, Homewood, Illinois; Richard D. Irwin, Inc., 1960.

Murphey, Rhoads, *An Introduction to Geography*, Chicago; Rand McNally and Company, 1961.

Myer, John N., *Accounting for Non-Accountants*, Rye, New York; American Research Council, 1964.

Neuner, John J. W. and B. Lewis Keeling, *Administrative Office Management*, Cincinnati; South Western Publishing Company, 1966.

Newman, William H. and Charles E. Summer, Jr., *The Process of Management: Concepts, Behavior, and Practice*, Englewood Cliffs, New Jersey; Prentice-Hall, Inc., 1960.

Porter, Donald E. and Philip B. Applewhite, *Studies in Organizational Behavior and Management*. Scranton, Pennsylvania; International Textbook Company, 1964.

Rae, W. Fraser, *The Business of Travel*, London; Thomas Cook and Son, 1891.

Rugoff, Milton, *The Great Travelers* (Two Volumes), New York; Simon and Schuster, 1960.

Sales, H. Pearce, *Travel and Tourism Encyclopedia*, London; Blandford Press, 1959.

Schleier, Curt, "A Filing System that Works," *ASTA Travel News*, July, 1968.

Simonds, Rollin H., Richard E. Ball and Eugene J. Kelley, *Business Administration Problems and Functions*, Boston; Allyn and Bacon, Inc. 1962.

Smith, Richard E., "Good Accounting. . . First Step to Agency Profits," *ASTA Travel News*, January, 1968.

Terry, George R., *Principles of Management*, Fifth Edition, Homewood, Illinois; Richard D. Irwin, Inc. 1968.

Townsend, Robert, *Up the Organization*, New York; Alfred A. Knopf, 1970.

Pan American World Airways, Inc. gratefully acknowledges the assistance of the members of our Travel Agents Advisory Board whose knowledge, experience and professionalism provided the direction for this publication.

George G. Brownell, CTC, Brownell Tours, Birmingham, Alabama

Thomas J. Donovan, CTC, Cartan Travel Bureau, Inc., Chicago, Illinois

Lawrence J. Frommer, CTC, Frommer Travel Agency, Washington, D. C.

Bernard Garber, CTC, Garber's Travel Service, Inc., Brookline, Mass.

Gilbert D. Haroche, Liberty Travel Service, Inc., New York, N. Y.

Carl L. Helgren, CTC, Where-To-Go Travel Service, Inc., Seattle, Wash.

Robert W. Hemphill, CTC, Hemphill's Travel Service, Inc., Los Angeles, California

Charles Hiller, Hiller Travel Service, Inc., New York, N. Y.

Robert H. Jackson, CTC, Jackson Travel Agency, Inc., Tyler, Texas

Thomas M. Keesling, CTC, Travel Associates, Inc., Englewood, Colorado

Milton A. Marks, CTC, Marks Travel Service, Dayton, Ohio

James A. Miller, CTC, Waldo Travel Agency, Inc., East Lansing, Michigan

Arnold C. Rigby, CTC, Arnold Tours, Inc., Boston, Massachusetts

Nancy J. Stewart, CTC, Hyde Travel Service, Inc., Pittsburgh, Pennsylvania

Charles G. Tilbury, Beverly Hills Travel Bureau, Inc., Beverly Hills, California

ABOUT THE AUTHORS

Robert W. McIntosh
Editor and Co-Author of Chapter 1
The Travel Agency Business

Robert W. McIntosh is a Professor at the School of Hotel, Restaurant and Institutional Management and Specialist in Tourist and Resort Management at Michigan State University. Dr. McIntosh was Chairman of the Governor's Task Force Committee report on tourist development in 1959 (Michigan's Governor G. Mennen Williams). He is the author of many books and articles on the tourist and resort industry, motel management and travel agency operations. He is a consultant to the Italian Government Tourism Promotion Bureau and to ICTA, and was appointed educational consultant to the International Union of Official Travel Organizations at Geneva. Dr. McIntosh has been active with the Conservation Institute of Michigan State, and is a member of the Dean's Committee for the Center for Environmental Quality. He has received awards from professional, educational and civic groups for his work in the development and promotion of travel and the travel industry.

James A. Miller
Co-Author of Chapter 1
The Travel Agency Business

James A. Miller is President of Waldo Travel Agency, Inc., and Manager of College Travel Office in East Lansing, Michigan. During his 36 years of experience in the travel industry, he has held various positions with airlines, railroads and agencies. Mr. Miller is National Chairman of ASTA's Study Committee on Cooperatives and a member of the National Finance and Study Committee. He has been National Area Director for Michigan, Ohio, Indiana and Kentucky. As a Founder Trustee and National Secretary of ICTA, he has worked with Michigan State University's College of Business in the development of ICTA's educational and certifying materials. Mr. Miller is a member of the Detroit SKAL Club.

Carl Massara
Chapter 2
Office Layout and Design

Carl Massara is founder of Carl Massara and Associates, Architects in Philadelphia and Chairman of the Architectural Design and Construction Technology Department of Temple University's Technology Institute. He was awarded a Harvard Graduate School of Design Scholarship and in 1962 the Alpha Rho Chi Medal for leadership, merit and service in the field of architecture. His firm has completed a master planning study of an area of Santa Marta Bay on the island of Curacao, and has designed structures for historic Philadephia's Society Hill redevelopment.

Helen Hinkson Green
Chapter 3
Travel Agency Employees
Chapter 4
Organizing the Work

Helen Hinkson Green is a Professor at Michigan State University, dually appointed in the College of Business and the College of Education. She has written numerous professional articles and books, including the column "Just Between Us." which appeared in *Business Education World* from 1957 to 1969, and *The Business Teacher's Handbook,* published by McGraw-Hill. Her time on and off campus is spent in consulting and conference work with business teachers, professional associations, secretaries and private industry, as well as teaching. She is Associate Editor of National Association of Business Teacher publications and Editorial Associate of *Business Education World.*

231

Richard F. Cook
Chapter 5
Profit Planning through
Correct Accounting Practices
Chapter 6
Automation and the Future

Richard F. Cook owned and managed Elite Travel Service and was General Manager of Travelpower, Inc. in Milwaukee for a sixteen-year period. He has served on the ASTA staff as Director of Special Services and most recently as a consultant in the areas of management and marketing to travel agents, and to those companies who market through travel agents. Mr. Cook's work includes the areas of automation, research, accounting, agency seminars, marketing and agency training. He is a contributing editor of *ASTA Travel News*, where his feature "The Bottom Line" appears monthly. He is a member of ICTA, an Allied member of ASTA, and a member of SKAL Club.

Roger M. Stillman
Chapter 7
Communications Equipment

Roger M. Stillman is Vice President and co-founder of Stillman & Dolan, Inc., a telephone and communications consulting firm in Philadelphia. He began his interest and career in communications in Army training school, and later worked with the Bell Telephone Company as a consultant in their Marketing Department. In 1966 he and his partner established Stillman & Dolan, expanded now to offices in Philadelphia, Pittsburgh and Wilmington.

Walter J. Mathews
Chapter 8
Travel Agency Marketing

Walter J. Mathews is founder of Walter Mathews Associates in New York, specialists in providing marketing services to the travel industry. After attending the University of California, Yale and Navy post graduate school, he joined American Airlines, serving as Director of Marketing Plans. As Vice President of Michael John Associates, Mr. Mathews was involved with the planning and producing of meetings, conventions, and sales presentations. The Mathews company, founded in 1965, brings together people with the special talents to provide an imaginative solution to specific problems in any marketing area in the field of travel.

Paul S. Quinn
Chapter 9
Legal Considerations in
Travel Agency Management

Paul S. Quinn is a partner in the Washington law firm of Wilkinson, Cragun & Barker, and is primarily responsible for the firm's general counsel representation of ASTA. He is a graduate of Providence College and Georgetown Law Center. Mr. Quinn served as Legislative Assistant to United States Senator Claiborne Pell of Rhode Island, and since entering private practice has been involved in legal matters in the field of travel and tourism. He is the author of several articles and contributed to a special volume of *European Transport Law,* published in 1968, relating to legal liability of travel agents. He was a member of the United States delegation to the International Convention on Travel Agent Liability held in Brussels in April, 1970.

239

INDEX

241

INDEX

INDEX

243

INDEX

Book Number   5709